HOPE IN A DARK TIME

hope

HOPE IN A DARK TIME

hope

REFLECTIONS ON HUMANITY'S FUTURE

EDITED BY DAVID KRIEGER

FOREWORD BY ARCHBISHOP DESMOND TUTU

Capra Press
Memorable Books Since 1969
Santa Barbara

A Robert Bason Book
Published by Capra Press
815 De La Vina Street
Santa Barbara, CA 93101
www.caprapress.com

Cover by Keith Puccinelli
Book design by Kathleen Baushke
Body type is Stempel Schneider.

Library of Congress Cataloging-in-Publication Data

Hope in a dark time: reflections on humanity's future / edited by David
Krieger; foreword by Archbishop Desmond Tutu.— 1st ed.
        p. cm.
"A Robert Bason Book."
ISBN 1-59266-005-3 (pbk.) — ISBN 1-59266-006-1 (hardcover numbered)
— ISBN 1-59266-007-X (hardcover lettered)
    1. Peace. 2. Nuclear nonproliferation. 3. Democracy. 4. Human
    beings. 5. Hope. I. Krieger, David.
JZ5538 .H67 2003
303.6'6—dc21
                                2002013363

    Edition: 10 9 8 7 6 5 4 3 2

To all who,
despite the darkness or because of it,
choose hope and work for peace,
and especially to

Frank K. Kelly

an elder statesman for humanity,
who in his ninth decade continues to work daily
for a world of peace and justice
in which everyone has a seat at humanity's table

and

Wallace T. Drew

a man of uncommon decency and unshakable faith
that a better world is possible
if each of us will only do our part.

Great ideas, it has been said, come into the world as gently as doves. Perhaps then, if we listen attentively, we shall hear amid the uproar of empires and nations, a faint flutter of wings, a gentle stirring of life and hope. Some will say that this hope lies in a nation; others in a person. I believe rather that it is awakened, revived, nourished by millions of solitary individuals whose deeds and works every day negate frontiers and the crudest implications of history. As a result, there shines forth fleetingly the ever-threatened truth that each and every person, on the foundation of his or her own sufferings and joys, builds for all.

—*Albert Camus (1913–1960)*
Nobel Laureate in Literature

The People Beneath

At the center of the city
The people were incinerated
Becoming ashes in the wind
With glowing red edges,
No longer holding memories
But becoming memories and
Drifting with the clouds.

At the edges of the city
The people survived longer,
Holding memories of the moment
In their bones,
Which later became brittle,
And in their hearts.

The survivors were sorrowful
And did their best to remind us
Of the new elements in the wind,
But their voices were soft
And it was a busy time on Earth.

—David Krieger

Acknowledgments

Each of the authors in this volume is a dedicated peace builder. Without the significant efforts and contributions of these talented and dedicated individuals this volume would not exist.

We were fortunate to be supported in this project by Archbishop Desmond Tutu, who provided the Foreword, and by H.H. The Dalai Lama, who contributed the poem and important advice, "Never Give Up."

Many of the chapters in this volume originated in the work of the Nuclear Age Peace Foundation, whose board members, advisors, supporters and staff are dedicated to building a better future for all humanity.

Special thanks to Ilene Pritikin and Selma Rubin for proofreading, to Kathleen Baushke for typesetting, to Keith Pucinnelli for cover design, and to Bob Bason and Rich Barre of Capra Press for their support.

Finally, I want to thank my wife, Carolee, for her ongoing support and dedication to efforts such as this book to reach a broader public with messages of peace and individual empowerment.

Contents

Some Final Thoughts

Appendices

Foreword

By Archbishop Desmond Tutu

The message of this important book is that hope matters. Hope is not only the light that can be found at the end of the tunnel. It is also the light, faint and flickering though it may be, that can help us to navigate the darkness of our times. Hope is an inner light that can strengthen our resolve to create a better world.

Hope is also a gift we can share with our fellow humans. One person's hope can ignite hope in those who might be on the verge of succumbing to despair. Knowing this makes our hope a responsibility to ourselves and to our fellow humans with whom we share our lives.

I have lived through the dark days of apartheid, days that seemed endless in their unfairness as they undermined the dignity of both the oppressed and the oppressors. Through those dark days, the spark of hope kept us motivated to build a more decent society. Whoever would have thought that South Africa, once a pariah nation known throughout the world for its cruelty, could itself become a beacon of hope that constructive change is possible? And yet, this has happened within our lifetime.

The life of Nelson Mandela is a tribute to hope. That this man could endure 27 years of imprisonment, mostly in solitary confinement, and emerge with his spirit intact and his hope unimpaired is a beautiful testament to the human spirit. And in my country there have been many such testaments to the inherent dignity that resides at the core of our humanity.

Nelson Mandela's courage and hope have helped give hope to the world. But it is not only great leaders that can be a source of hope. Each of us has that power. Each person's hope can trigger a revolution of hope in friends and acquaintances. There is a powerful multiplier effect that springs forth from the hope of even a single individual.

I have had many blessings in my life. One of the greatest of these has been to witness the power of forgiveness. In the aftermath of the apartheid regime in South Africa, we chose the path of forgiveness and reconciliation. As the chair of the Truth and Reconciliation Commission, I learned first-hand the transformative nature of forgiveness. It is a power that can cleanse the human heart and free us from hatred and bloodlust. I am convinced there is no future without forgiveness, and in forgiveness there is hope that we can put an end to wars and violence.

We need each other. In Africa, we have a word, *ubuntu*, that means we can only be human together. I cannot be human without you being human. Our destinies are intertwined and we share a common humanity. To be fully human, we must work together, with each other and for each other. In *ubuntu*, there is hope that we can embrace our common humanity to create our common destiny.

This book brings together the thoughts of some of the world's most committed peacemakers. Each of the authors reflects upon humanity's future and shared destiny. The important message of this book that shines through its pages is that with hope all things are possible and that we must never allow ourselves to sink into despair and cynicism. Rather, the future is in our hands, and we must never cease our efforts to build the paradise on Earth that God intended us to have.

This book is a gift of love and a gift of peace. It can help us navigate through the fog of darkness that sometimes seems overwhelming. It can help us remember our common humanity and our common destiny, and it can inspire us to play our own special role in shaping the future and shining the light of hope around us.

:

Introduction

By David Krieger

H as there ever been a time when humanity's future has stood at greater risk? Large numbers of people live in despair, without adequate food, water or sanitation. We live in a world in which education and health care are beyond the reach of a significant percentage of the world's people. Despair is another word for hopelessness; it is a breeding ground for violence. Is it any wonder that wars continue throughout the world and that terrorism has become a part of the normal backdrop of living?

The response to these conditions in the small enclaves of the rich has been to try to build the castle walls higher and higher in the impossible effort to achieve invulnerability. The United States, for example, has tried to build the castle walls so high that they cover the sky. It calls this effort its missile defense program and pours tens of billions of dollars into a program that has no realistic possibility of success.

Terrorists will not attack with missiles; rather, they will find ways to go around or under the castle walls. They will devise simple schemes to make a mockery of this technological dream of invulnerability. There are no castle walls that can be built high enough or strong enough to assure security for the "haves" while much of the world slips further into the depths of despair.

It is a luxury to be able to think about humanity's future. Most people in the world are utterly consumed by the struggle simply to stay alive. Even among those people who do have the time and opportunity to think about the bigger picture, many choose not to do so. It is not a priority because they have a false sense of security behind the castle walls and often are too engaged in the diversions of entertainment made possible by wealth.

Whatever the cause, there is a widespread failure to understand that the greatest enemies of humanity's future are our tools of destruction, our weapons of war and annihilation, to which we have become addicted. Equally powerful enemies are ignorance and apathy, seemingly pervasive maladies of our time. They have afflicted the masses of people and, not surprisingly, found their way into the highest offices in democracies as well as dictatorships.

Humanity faces enormous challenges and it is no wonder that some people question whether there are any rational reasons for hope. But reasons for hope do not need to be rational. Hope may be wildly irrational. Perhaps, given the state of the world today, hope must be irrational. But rational or irrational, hope is a blessing and a grounding for acts that still may save us in these critical times.

Is there hope? Each of us must find his or her own answer to this question. This book both asks this question and answers it in the affirmative. Of course, there is hope. There is hope because there is the uniquely human capacity for hope and because we know intuitively and from experience that human beings are able to work together in building a better world.

Hope, says Vaclav Havel, "is an orientation of the heart; it transcends the world that is immediately experienced, and is anchored somewhere beyond its horizons." Hope leads us to risk believing that tomorrow can be different from today, that we have the possibility of creating a more decent future for ourselves and for humanity.

Hope is a place of new beginnings. It provides perspective on what is possible. It can open our eyes and our hearts to new vistas of possible futures. It is a key ingredient of vision, seeing that the future can be far more than simply a straight-line projection of the past. Hope provides energy for participating in creating a future that corresponds to our dreams. Without hope, we might not even dare to dream.

Walls separate us, whether they are castle walls, borders, or the boundaries of our imaginations. Our hope lies in overcoming these walls and finding the common ground of our humanity, ground where humanity can meet on terms of equity and human dignity. This is the ground we must find if there is to be hope for humanity's future. This is the ground where seeds of peace, cooperation and human dignity can be planted and nurtured. Already there are millions of people throughout the world seeking this ground, planting seeds and nurturing seedlings of hope.

We all have choices. We can build walls or we can build bridges. We can give our talents to creating weapons of annihilation, as so many scientists have done, or we can work to find solutions to humanity's greatest problems. Our orientation is found not only in our acts, but also in the policies we support or oppose.

Each of us matters. The world is created by the sum of our actions or inactions. Albert Einstein wrote, "The world is a dangerous place to live, not because of the people who are evil, but because of the people who don't do anything about it." In the end, the worst that we can do is nothing. This will assure the triumph of evil and possibly the end of civilization and even of our species.

The Earth can survive without us. In geological time, human civilization is a newcomer to Earth. If we destroy everything that we have created—all the great music, literature, art, architecture and philosophy—the Earth will go on. It is these treasures and the memories, the beauty, the love, and the future that are worth fighting for, as we resist the world's drift towards self-destruction.

I have to imagine that Gandhi had hope when he set out on his march to the sea to repeal the British salt tax, that Nelson Mandela had hope as he sat for seemingly endless days and years in prison, and that Martin Luther King, Jr. had hope as he marched in Selma, Alabama and as he delivered his great "I Have a Dream" speech on the steps of the US Capitol. I have to imagine that Rosa Parks had hope when she refused to give up her seat and move to the back of the bus. Hope is a catalyst for change that gives birth to dreams and to action.

But hope without conviction and action is like a still pool. It may reflect, but it goes nowhere. Hope is not enough to change the world, to bring peace, to end starvation and poverty, to provide a decent education for all children, or to prevent nuclear holocaust. Yet, it is a critical starting point for building a better and brighter future. All of us are challenged to connect hope to action until we have created a mighty river that will carve a new path to the future.

In this book, an extraordinary group of visionaries explore their hopes for humanity's future. Each of the authors has dedicated his or her life to building a better future for humanity. They are not simply optimists. They are talented dreamers and activists who daily contribute their visions and their lives to building a better world.

I believe that all of the authors share an understanding that humanity is endangered as never before and that the futures of our families, our communities, our nations, and the common future of humanity stand in jeopardy. They share in the belief that our times compel extraordinary efforts to achieve a more just and decent future for all, and thereby necessitate greater efforts to achieve peace and security.

This book is an invitation to hope and to action. It is an invitation to set aside the obstacles to action, to choose peace and to *wage peace*. It is an invitation to help shape humanity's future.

HOPE IN A DARK TIME

hope

hope
IS THERE HOPE?

Creating a New Future

By Bill Cane

A Quechua Indian friend of mine once told me that the phrase "The future is ahead of you" made no sense to him. "We can see what is ahead of us," he insisted. "It's what is behind us that we cannot see. For the Quechua, the future is always behind us."

Look ahead as we may, we cannot see the future. What we can see are past and present trends—environmental disaster approaching, the gap between the rich and the poor widening, and weapons of destruction proliferating. If we project any one of these trends into the future, the outlook is grim indeed.

People Create the Future

Thank God that trends and statistical projections do not create the future. People do. And people who go against the trends can create a future that is very different from the past.

"Some people have to come too early," wrote philosopher-historian Eugen Rosenstock-Huessy, "so that others can arrive on time." People who envision a different future can create a radically new story on the earth. The ability to create the future is a participation in divinity. "We should recognize as God's specific quality in us the power to break away from the established order of mind and body and create a new future," wrote Rosenstock-Huessy.

History attests to humanity's ability to go against prevailing trends. When historian Page Smith began writing his eight-volume *People's*

History of the United States, he felt that he might, like Gibbon, be describing the rise and fall of an empire. "But by volume four," he tells us, "I had cheered myself up considerably." What cheered him was the continual and unexpected emergence of reform movements in American history.

"When you know of the trials and tribulations of people in American history, and when you see history as a tragic drama, as I do—and against this backdrop, you still see the patience, the faith and persistence with which some people have pursued some higher vision—when you see this over decades and generations, then I think hope is inevitable," wrote Smith.

He felt that kindling and passing on a spirit of hope is at the heart of history. His favorite story began with Abraham Lincoln and the Abolition Movement. Lincoln had a friend whom he called "good old double-d'd Addams." Addams' daughter Jane came home one day to find her father crying. "The greatest man in the world has been killed," he sobbed. Lincoln had been assassinated. As a privileged young woman, Jane Addams went through a period of deep depression. But she soon was to find her life's vocation when she saw people fighting over rotten vegetables in the slums of London. She returned to the US to found a series of settlement houses where poor immigrants could find understanding and support in their new country. Twenty-five years later, when Myles Horton wanted to bring the blacks and whites of the South together, he went to visit Jane Addams. Much impressed, Myles went back to Tennessee and founded Highlander Folk School. Another twenty-five years went by and Myles Horton phoned Martin Luther King, Sr. to ask if anyone in his congregation might benefit from a session at Highlander. King suggested a woman named Rosa Parks. Six weeks after Rosa Parks left Highlander, she refused to step to the back of the bus.

Keeping the Spirit of Hope Alive

From Abraham Lincoln to Rosa Parks—from the Emancipation Proclamation to the Civil Rights movement—is about 100 years. And over that span, the spirit of the Abolition movement ebbed and flowed, at times all but disappearing. But we can trace a spirit being kept alive and passed on from Lincoln to Addams to Jane Addams to Myles Horton to Rosa Parks. And that is what history is all about—the passing on of a spirit from one generation to the next, keeping that spirit of human hope alive (even in the darkest of times) until it breaks out again to give new life to the larger society.

We cannot tell when that spirit is going to break out. Rosenstock-Huessy saw history as the story of unlikely events that seemed to arise out of nowhere. "History," he wrote, "tells us of the unbeliev-able creation of new events, because not only are they new, but they are unbelievable before they have happened.... It is impossible by reason to prove that anything new can ever happen.... Every-body said that people could not fly until Orville Wright did fly. Then of course they said, 'We knew it all the time. It is so simple.'"

When I get discouraged about the future, I try to recall the sur-prises of the recent past. Less than twenty-five years ago people tore the Berlin wall down. The Solidarity movement transformed Poland. The Filipino people ousted Marcos. Nelson Mandela be-came president of South Africa.

"*Auctoritas in senatu, potestas in populo*" was an old Roman saying. "The senate has authority but the people have power." Hannah Arendt adds that the people have power insofar as they stay orga-nized and keep at it. If they do not, bureaucracies, which are perma-nently organized, take the people's power away from them.

Even the poorest of the poor have changed their future by com-ing together and keeping at it. In Brazil the organization Sem Terra began with landless peasants. Thousands of people spend a year or more in training, and then decide if they are ready to occupy a piece of unused land. They move secretly at night—four or five thousand at a time. They occupy the land and wait for the army to surround them, trusting that their large numbers will preclude acts of vio-lence against them. They can negotiate with the government be-cause Brazil's constitution allows people to occupy land that has lain unused for a certain number of years. Hundreds of thousands of people have acquired land through Sem Terra, and those who already have land provide food and support for new occupants.

7

The *comedores*, or women's kitchens, in Peru began with poor women from the Andes who had moved to Lima and could not afford to feed their families. They began to group together. Ten women cook for one hundred families, leaving the other women free to care for children or get little jobs. The women learn to buy in bulk, to organize, to conduct their own elections. Today, over 500,000 meals are served each day in and around Lima. The women of the *comedores* have become a political force.

THE FUTURE BEGAN YESTERDAY

In small ways, human beings are at work all over the planet, planting the seeds of a hope-filled future. The future began yesterday. There are nuclear-free countries, nuclear-free zones, and a host of people working for a nuclear-free world. The movement to ban landmines has made great progress. Practically every country on earth has an organized peace movement. Peace Brigades International—a group which accompanies popular leaders who are under death threat—keeps growing.

The protests at Seattle and at subsequent World Trade Organization meetings attest to strong movements for democratic control of agriculture and of natural resources worldwide. Food First and similar organizations in many countries continue to fight for food as a human right. The European Union is itself a minor miracle, and it has made great strides in supporting the economies of the poorer member nations rather than keeping them down. In the United States, unions, religious leaders, community leaders and environmentalists are forming local coalitions to work for a sustainable society.

Technologies for sustainability keep springing up. Organic agriculture grows more sophisticated and stronger every year. John Todd and Ocean Arks International keep developing "living machines" for natural disposal of wastes and sewage. In their new experiments they are completing the circle of recycling so that waste eventually becomes food. We have more and more models of environmental buildings and environmental communities. Germany is phasing out its nuclear power plants and replacing them with offshore wind power. Flywheels that are virtually frictionless are being used to store photovoltaic electricity. Hydrogen fuel cells show real promise as sources of non-polluting energy.

The New World Order, however, is designed not to serve people or the environment but the interests of multinational corporations. At the present moment money and corporate power have largely taken over the government of the United States. The US arms budget is now larger than the combined military budgets of many countries. Corporate and military control seem complete. But suddenly little cracks appear. Enron dramatizes how corporate greed and government corruption collude, and campaign finance reform finally achieves a legislative victory.

WE EACH HAVE OUR PART TO PLAY

If we demand immediate results, we will easily be discouraged. A hopeful future is the work of generations. We have to reach back and grasp the hands of those who have gone before us and encourage younger people who are coming after us. The work will never cease. In Lord Acton's words: "Everything good has to be done over and over again forever."

No one of us has control of the whole. We have only our small part to play. Visionary William Blake saw the value of doing small things: "Those who do good must do so in minute particulars. The general good is the plea of the scoundrel and the hypocrite." When it seems impossible to change the larger picture, we must focus on minute particulars. Wendell Berry is suspicious of those who desire to change the whole world at once. People who have thought globally, he remarks, have done a lot of damage! So he too suggests that we think locally—work hard to preserve the local economy, small business, the small farmer, our natural resources and the productivity of our land.

THE POWER OF PERSONAL COMMUNICATION

A democratic future demands that people's voices be heard, that artists and musicians and authors and dancers ("Beauty," Dostoevski wrote, "may save the world") and the people in the streets and on the farms have their say. However, the world's mainstream media is now controlled by only six mega-corporations. Corporate and government agendas dominate our mainstream news, and the stories of people who are creating alternatives to those agendas are largely ignored. In such a climate it becomes crucial to seek out alternative sources of news, to support local artists and local voices and to communicate good news ourselves. Dorothy Day, founder of the Catholic Worker Houses, was constantly sending articles and personal letters to friends to let them know what was really happening.

We must never underestimate the power of personal communication. In Eastern Europe under Communism, dissidents used carbon paper and hand-copying to disseminate their vision of a different future. We are blessed with e-mail, copy machines and an array of alternative publications.

Standing Up for Spiritual Values

In an increasingly money-oriented world, we need to stand up for spiritual values. The economy and the bottom line have become our gods. We have come to rely on "the economy." For most of our history, however, the word "economy" was used exclusively for the distribution of grace—"the economy of salvation." What mattered was faith and hope and love flowing through the society and being passed from person to person. What mattered was the karma being accumulated by our actions. Gandhi was fond of pointing out that no social system will work unless the people are good. Grace and karma and our support of one another in community still matter vitally. That is where our real security lies.

Going against the prevailing story involves sacrifice. A willingness to sacrifice may well be a prerequisite for a hopeful future. The apostle Paul seems to have felt so: "We rejoice even in our afflictions, because affliction gives rise to endurance and endurance to character and character to hope. And this hope does not let us down

10

because the love of God has been poured forth into our hearts by the spirit given to us."

THE SPIRIT OF LOVE ENDURES

The spirit of love endures beyond our individual lifetimes. Many years ago, I spent time with Bill Hamlet, a San Francisco police inspector who was dying from cancer. We had both been involved with the deaf community in San Francisco, and Bill asked that at his funeral his arms be crossed over his heart to form the deaf sign for love. His last silent message to all of us was that love endures beyond death.

That is our greatest hope—that love will prevail. "The history of the human race," Rosenstock-Huessy wrote, "is written on a single theme: How does Love become stronger than Death? The composition is recomposed in each generation by those whose love overcomes murdering or dying. So history becomes a great song.... As often as the lines rhyme, love has once again become stronger than death.... This rhyming, this connecting, is our function on earth."

The Great Turning

By Joanna Macy

A revolution is underway. And, in the words of Gil Scott Heron, this "revolution will not be televised." It is not featured in the mainstream press either. Corporate-controlled media are blind to it. But once you become aware of this tidal change, it will make you glad to be alive. Our time in history will appear to you, not as some grim, hopeless fate in which we are trapped, but as a great adventure that can invigorate and ennoble every aspect of life.

What is this adventure? It is the epochal shift from the industrial growth society to a life-sustaining society. And it is a matter of survival.

This revolution begins with the acknowledgment of two facts. First, an economic system that depends on ever-increasing corporate profits—on how fast the Earth can be turned into consumer goods, weapons, and waste—is suicidal. And second, our needs can be met without destroying our world. We have available technology and resources to produce sufficient food and energy, ensure clean air and water, and leave a livable world for those who come after us.

Future generations, if we allow them the means to exist, will look back on these beginning years of the twenty-first century, and they may well call this time the "Great Turning." I imagine they will say, "Those ancestors back then, bless them. Though involved in the Great Turning, they had no way of knowing whether they could pull it off. It must have looked hopeless at times. Their efforts must have often seemed isolated, paltry and darkened by confusion; yet they went ahead, they kept on doing what they could—and, because they did, the Great Turning happened."

An Ecological Revolution

A good number of us today are already using that term, the Great Turning. And many realize that it is comparable in magnitude to two other revolutions in human history. The first one, some 8000 years ago, was the agricultural revolution and it took centuries to unfold. The second, arising some 250 years ago, was the industrial revolution, and that took generations. Now, right on its heels, as the industrial growth society spins out of control, comes this *ecological* revolution. And because we are already exceeding the limits of what the Earth can restore and absorb—in systems terms, our economy is on "overshoot" and exponential "runaway"—this revolution must happen not in centuries or generations, but within a matter of years. At the same time, it must be more thorough-going—involving not only our institutions and technologies, but also the attitudes and habits that sustain them.

Now this runaway system cannot be corrected with the tools and mindsets we are accustomed to employ. Scientists see more clearly than politicians that there is no technological fix. No magic bullet can save us from cropland erosion, deforestation, poison by pollution, wholesale extinctions of plant and animal species, climate disruptions and consequent famines—or even nuclear war. That is because our political economy is harnessed to growth: it sets its goals and measures its performance by how fast corporate profits can increase. To save ourselves, we will have to change the rules, shift our goals. We will have to want different things, seek different pleasures, pursue different aims, than those that have been driving us and our global economy.

New values and new ways of meeting our needs must arise *now*, while we still have room to maneuver—and that is precisely what is happening. They are emerging at this very moment, like green shoots through the rubble of a dysfunctional society. If you open your eyes and fiddle with the focal length of your vision, you can almost *see* them—like a faint green haze over things, intensifying here and there in pools and pockets of grass, cress, clover.

No Guarantee

Before describing these green shoots of the Great Turning, let's pause to acknowledge that it may fail. There is no way to know if the Great Turning will happen fast enough or fully enough to stop the unraveling of our life support systems. There is no guarantee that we will make this transition in time for civilization, humanity, or even complex life forms, to survive.

When you make peace with that reality, you find a kind of liberation. You are freed from bracing yourself against every piece of bad news, and from having constantly to work up a sense of hopefulness in order to act—which can be exhausting. There is a certain equanimity and moral economy that comes when you are not constantly computing your chances of success. The enterprise is so vast, there is no way to judge the effects of this or that individual effort—or the extent to which it makes any difference at all. Once we acknowledge this, we are free to enjoy the adventure and the challenge. Then we can see it as a privilege, to be alive now, in this Great Turning, when all the wisdom and courage we ever harvested can be put to use and matter supremely.

Three Dimensions of the Great Turning

Let us look at how the Great Turning is happening. It unfolds in three simultaneous and mutually reinforcing dimensions. Recognize how they are impinging on your own life, gaining momentum through the choices you make and the visions you nourish.

I. *The most visible of these dimensions is holding actions in defense of life on Earth. This is what is generally considered to be "activism."*
Here we find all the political, legislative, legal, and regulatory work undertaken to slow down the destruction inflicted by the industrial growth society. Here we find direct actions as well—

blockades, boycotts, civil disobedience, and other forms of refusal. Often confronting active opposition from government and industry, this dimension includes:

- Resistance to pesticides, forest clearcutting, genetically modified foods, nuclear dumping.

- Campaigning for laws to mitigate pollution and loss of habitat, such as the Clean Water Act and the Endangered Species Act.

- Citizen monitoring, litigation, and participation in public hearings for enforcement of social and environmental regulations.

- Blowing the whistle on illegal and unethical corporate practices, and boycotting corporations that endanger living systems or exploit their workers with low pay and harmful working conditions.

- Providing shelter and food to the poor and the homeless.

- Protesting against global arms trade and abrogation of arms control and nuclear test ban treaties.

Work of this kind buys time. It saves lives, it saves some species, ecosystems and cultures, it preserves some of the gene pool for the sustainable society to come. Although insufficient by itself to bring that society about, it is necessary to the preservation of life.

Let's face it, this first dimension is wearing. You can get stressed out of your mind by nonstop crises, the constant search for funding, the battles lost, and the increasing violence against activists. When you step back to take a breather, you often feel as if you are abandoning ship. But to the extent you still care what's happening to the world, you're just slipping back to continue the work of the Great Turning in another form—the way the head goose, when she's tired, slips back and flies in the windstream of others, and another flyer takes her place.

II. *The second dimension of the Great Turning involves systems change. It addresses structural causes of the global crisis and creates sustainable alternatives.*

To free ourselves and our planet from the industrial growth society, we must understand its dynamics. What are the political and economic structures that lead us to use our Earth as supply house and sewer? What are the tacit agreements creating obscene wealth for a few, while the majority of humanity sinks into grueling poverty? A few years ago, it was hard slogging to raise public interest in GATT (Global Agreement on Trade and Tariffs) or NAFTA (North American Free Trade Agreement); people's eyes glazed over. But now, as an upsurge of books, articles, teach-ins and demonstrations demystifies the workings of the global economy, we are wising up. Informed public attention is widespread and lively.

Clarity as to how the old system works helps us see how it can change and be replaced. Alternative institutions and ways of doing things are mushrooming, from local currencies to local consumer cooperatives, from ecovillages to CSA's (community-supported agriculture). At no other epoch of human history have so many new ways of doing things appeared in so short a time. They may *look* marginal to us today, but they hold the seeds of the future. A few more examples:

- New measures of wealth and prosperity, sustainability indicators to replace the Gross Domestic Product, which ignores ecological and human health.

- A growing shift toward renewable energy based on wind, solar, and biomass technologies.

- New forms of land ownership such as land trusts and conservancies.

- Co-housing, ecovillages, and other new forms for creating community while building ecologically.

- Holistic health practices that acknowledge the self-healing capacities of body and mind.

- Permaculture, biodynamic farming, urban gardens, and other healthy, sustainable ways of growing food.

III. *These nascent forms will not survive, however, unless they are deeply rooted in values and attitudes. They must mirror what we want and how we experience our relations to Earth and each other. They require, in other words, a profound shift in our perception of reality.*

That paradigmatic shift—the third dimension of the Great Turning—is happening all around us. We are becoming aware of the web of relationships in which we have our being. We are helped by new discoveries in science, revealing that Earth is not inert matter to be used as a commodity, but a living system in which we are intricately embedded and interconnected. This cognitive revolution is paralleled by a spiritual revolution. Ancient teachings become available to us now, showing us the beauty and power that can be ours as conscious, responsible members of the living body of Earth. Like our primordial ancestors, we begin again to see the world as our body, and, whether we say the word or not, as sacred.

The forms of this awakening are many. Among them are:

- Cognitive frameworks, such as deep ecology, living systems theory, Gaia theory, and the "universe story", which, based in physics and biology, reveal the radical interconnectedness of all life.

- Spiritual perspectives and practices drawn from life-affirming currents within the major religions of East and West, as well as from Earth-wisdom traditions of native peoples.

- The simple living, or voluntary simplicity movement, which liberates people from patterns of consumption that do not reflect their true needs, and brings them more satisfying ways of connecting with their world.

- New practices and rituals to affirm our mutual belonging in the web of life, and to nourish courage and solidarity as we work together for the Great Turning.

These new ways of seeing and celebrating engender a shift in consciousness, which can free us from the grip of the industrial growth society. They offer us nobler goals and truer pleasures. They help preserve us from paralysis or panic, when things are hard, so that we can resist the temptation to either stick our heads in the sand or seek scapegoats for our fears. They help us move forward with trust in ourselves and each other, so that we can join hands in learning how the world self-heals.

THE SHIFT TO A LIFE-SUSTAINING CIVILIZATION

As we reflect on these three dimensions of the Great Turning, we can recognize how they are stirring our hearts and lives, and the lives of countless brothers and sisters. The great adventure is underway. The epochal shift to a life-sustaining civilization is a reality. Granted, there is no guarantee we can pull it off in time. We cannot tell which will happen first: the final unraveling of complex life-forms on Earth, or the moment when the elements of a sustainable civilization cohere and catch hold. But without that gamble, could we discover the full measure of our courage? Could our own, wild creativity be really unleashed?

When the times we are living in seem apocalyptic, it is good to remember the true meaning of that word. Though "apocalypse" came to connote disaster, it originally meant revelation, disclosure. The very crises confronting us now, with all their horrors and apparent hopelessness, can disclose our true nature. They can reveal who and what we really are. Then it dawns on us that, even if the Great Turning "fails," it can still be our greatest moment. For it awakens us to our mutual belonging in the living body of Earth, and the joy of working together, in league with all beings.

Reasons for Hope in a Turbulent World

BY SENATOR DOUGLAS ROCHE, O.C.

On September 11, 1990, President George H.W. Bush, described the emergence of a New World Order, forecasting an unparalleled era of cooperation and advancement between states:

> ...a new era—freer from the threat of terror, stronger in the pursuit of justice, and more secure in the quest for peace, an era in which the nations of the world, East and West, North and South, can prosper and live in harmony.[1]

There was good reason for hope. The fall of the Berlin Wall had signalled the end of the Cold War, the "Iron Curtain" was pulled back across Europe, and the threat of nuclear annihilation seemed like a distant nightmare. The Warsaw Pact disintegrated and the very existence of NATO, its Western counterpart, was thrown into question as military budgets declined. With conflict looming in the Persian Gulf, the United Nations was able to assume the role its creators had envisioned, and a multinational coalition successfully removed Saddam Hussein from Kuwait. Despite an initially slow start, Western economies grew with unprecedented endurance. After years of deficits, governments suddenly had to decide how to disperse tax cuts and how to spend huge budget surpluses. The major economies of Western Europe and North America merged into free-trade zones and opportunity seemed limitless. Being optimistic about the future was definitely in fashion.

Eleven years to the day later, on September 11, 2001, our optimism was shattered. Instead of a New World Order, President George W. Bush began to talk of a world divided between those who support terrorism and those who work with the United States to defeat it. Rather than envisioning "a new world order where diverse nations are drawn together in common cause to achieve the universal aspirations of mankind—peace and security, freedom, and the rule of law,"[2] the current President sees "an axis of evil, arming to threaten the peace of the world."[3] As the U.S. pushes ahead with its "war on terrorism," the buoyancy that accompanied the end of the Cold War has disappeared. The terrorist attacks served as a reminder that the world is not out of the dark yet.

A Violent Wake-Up Call

September 11, 2001, was a violent wake-up call that served to draw our attention to a phenomenon hidden from sight by the Cold War and largely undetected by presidents and commentators alike. While the superpower rivalry gripped the world, a global society was burgeoning in which states were no longer the only—or even the primary—components. Led by changes in technologies for the movement of people, materials, and information, power has been shifting from governments to groups and individuals. As September 11 reminded us, not all of these actors have peaceful intentions; rather, they use their new-found power toward selfish and often violent ends. Combined with the lifting of old Cold War restraints, this system has spread at an unprecedented rate, bringing increased complexity and unpredictability with it.

The terrorists brutally drew our attention to our increased vulnerability. For this is the case when a small group of minimally armed terrorists can wreak havoc against the most powerful nation. The violent attacks against the U.S. brought home the realization that even a superpower is unable to protect its citizens from the purveyors of violence in this new era.

Other societies have known this reality for some time. The world of fear and uncertainty suddenly thrust upon the West has been commonplace reality for a large proportion of the planet's population for some time. Although seldom analyzed by the mainline media, threats to individual security have reached epidemic proportions. Civil conflict, drugs, AIDS, landmines, ethnic cleansing, famine, environmental disaster and poverty are just a few of the perils that are commonplace existence for much of humanity. Just as a market crash in Thailand can reverberate in Brazil, so too can the discontent of relatively few be expressed violently in the heart of America.

Looking at globalization through such a lens, there would seem to be little reason for optimism. But the same international system that has provided fertile ground for violence and misery also provides the basis for advancement and countless reasons for hope. Groundbreaking discoveries in technology have served to produce larger, more integrated, and more efficient markets. Increased levels of trade have made us richer and have enabled us to lead more diverse lives. Globalization has fostered information exchange, led to a greater understanding of other cultures, and allowed democracy to reign over autocracy. The new technologies have served to catalyze the growth of civil society, provide the glue for its cohesiveness, and amplify its collective voice on a whole range of issues stretching from the communal to the international level. Globalization is indeed a two-way street. Yet, as September 11, 2001, reminded us, it is perilous to adopt an attitude of complacency and overconfidence toward it. In fact, we have only a rudimentary understanding of this new era and even less control over it. At the same time, we must not underestimate our capacity to assemble the knowledge and innovation we need to make the best of it.

The question is not one of accepting or rejecting globalization. It is here to stay and to try to stop it would entail a huge cost to human development. Rather, as we understand and learn to navigate the new system we have suddenly found ourselves in, the question confronting us is one of management and innovation. Simply put, we must manage the system in a way that benefits the most people while inflicting the least amount of harm. At the same time, thanks to advances in technology and understanding, we have it in our power to produce widespread prosperity and social justice.

Understandably, the contradictions, disparities and despair that characterize globalization are the source of much confusion and make it very difficult to find reasons for hope. But, the fact is, hope lies in the blossoming of intelligence about ourselves as a human community in a world that is interconnected in every sphere of activity. This is an empowering discovery, capable of elevating the public policy process above the headlines and beyond the day-to-day preoccupations of governments.

GLOBALIZATION: THE GOOD, THE BAD AND THE UGLY

If the Cold War was about division, balance of power politics and definable enemies, this new era of globalization is all about integration, power diffusion and threats from enemies that are neither readily apparent nor definable. Driven by dramatic changes in technology, the new system is unprecedented in its pace, scope, and complexity. As the foreign affairs columnist for *The New York Times*, Thomas Friedman, explains in his book, *The Lexus and the Olive Tree*, globalization is an unstoppable process whereby markets, countries and technology have come together in such a way as to enable individuals, corporations and countries to reach around the world in ways never before thought possible.[4] Combined with the dismantling of the walls that defined the Cold War system, this process was only unleashed in the past decade. Since the transition is only beginning, many of the attitudes and methods that underpinned the old system are still very much with us.

THE GOOD

Looking at it through an economic point of view, globalization is about the spread—indeed the flood—of free market capitalism to every corner of the world. With advances in technology and a corresponding drop in its cost, more countries are able to produce more products more cheaply and participate in markets they were effectively excluded from before. When a country starts producing more products and lowers economic barriers, capital tends to flow in. As the logic goes, the more one opens up one's economy to free trade and competition, the more efficient and wealthy one will become. The invisible hand championed by the eighteenth century political economist, Adam Smith, is seen to do a pretty good job. Individuals choose what serves their own self-interest, each making an autonomous decision, the ultimate result being that every country advances and benefits. It is certainly true that globalization has made a welcomed contribution to reducing poverty in some of the largest and strongest economies, including China, India, and some of the Asian Tigers.

More than simply facilitating trade and investment, new technologies have also been the driving force behind sweeping advances in communication and information services, and progress made in the natural sciences. Because globalization involves the wiring of vast networks around the world, individuals and groups have the power to influence both markets and states in unprecedented ways. A groundbreaking achievement inaugurating this new reality was the 1997 signing of the Canada-led Anti-Personnel Landmine Treaty. With few other states supporting her, despite opposition by the major powers, Jody Williams—a Vermont activist—was able to use the Internet in putting together an international coalition of more than 1,000 civil society organizations to apply sufficient pressure on states to force policy change. Her efforts won her the Nobel Peace Prize. This multi-track exercise has since proven successful in achieving the Rome Treaty establishing the International Criminal Court (ICC). In this instance, a similar coalition of civil society groups and international law experts proved key in promoting acceptance of the ICC. Using information technologies, these groups were able to better convey the importance of international justice and make it a priority for governments.

In the same way, technological revolutions are bringing about numerous advances in biotechnology, genetics, astrophysics and other sciences that are revolutionizing our perception of life and the world surrounding us. The cracking of the genetic code and progress in genetic engineering is clearing the path for new gene therapies to treat formerly incurable genetically transmitted diseases. Research being done with stem cells holds great promise in treating a whole range of illness. Indeed, reading the front page of the paper, it would seem as if globalization is synonymous with boundless prosperity and progress and a clear step forward for humanity. However, judging by the surge in anti-globalization protests and the uncertainty left in the wake of September 11, 2001, the new era promises to be a turbulent one.

THE BAD AND THE UGLY

In fact, this is already the case. The same forces behind economic prosperity, civil society empowerment and scientific advance also serve to complicate an already confusing situation. A driver of economic growth on the one hand, globalization is perhaps a more powerful driver of inequality, injustice and conflict. This side of globalization must be recognized and acknowledged if we are to direct the advances and benefits of the new era to their widest benefit and truly advance as a global civilization.

With regard to economics, the market ignores the necessity of social justice. Equitable economic and social development has not been the critical issue as countries have sought larger markets, but the dramatic rise in trade and investment has suddenly thrust the issue onto political agendas. Globalization has served to widen the gulf between the rich and poor. It is a highly differentiated and unequal process, which in its current state does not involve full and complete integration of all nations into the "new economy" or a "new deal" for development at the global level. Globalization is not as "global" as supposed. The United States, like other industrialized countries, sends most of its outward foreign direct investment to other rich countries. By the late 1990s, around 80 percent of U.S. foreign direct investment was in Canada, Japan, and Western Europe, with 19 percent going to middle-income developing countries, including Brazil, Mexico, Indonesia, and Thailand, and barely 1 percent going to the poorest developing countries.[5] Trade ratios reflect a similar trend. Economic activity is directed to where it can be expected to maximize profits in the short-term with little regard for longer-term investment objectives including education, health, and peacebuilding. It is also true that the most lucrative trade revolves around armaments and militaries—a business worth $800 billion in 2000.[6]

Further, the rapid expansion in the quest for profit has served to widen this divide between the world's haves and have-nots. Although it is true that the incomes of the poor have risen alongside those of the wealthy, globalization of trade and finance has done little to narrow the gap between them.[7] This skewed distribution of wealth at the global level has been characterized by great stability, and there is no foreseeable change in this trend. Despite a narrowing of relative differences between many countries, the overall difference between developing countries and Organization for Economic Cooperation and Development (OECD) countries has widened in many regions. The fastest growing region, East Asia and the Pacific, has seen the difference between its income and that of OECD countries expand from about $6,000 in 1960 to more than $13,000 in 1998.[8] Between 1970 and 1990, the gulf between the world's richest and poorest increased two-fold from less than $9,000 per person to nearly $18,000 per person.[9] Based on current trends, the United Nations Development Programme predicts the disparity between the top and bottom fifths of countries will be more than 100-fold in 2025 and 200-fold by 2050. The story is similar within countries. With inequality comes an erosion of social capital—especially in the sense of the trust and civic responsibility that is vital to the establishment and sustainability of solid public institutions.

The prospects for a peaceful and constructive civil society are similarly discouraging. Civil society is not always "civil." The same technological advances that have empowered peace activists have also served to strengthen more devious forces. The lowering of economic barriers along with the declining cost of transportation and information technologies have been a boon for illicit arms merchants, drug traffickers, money launderers, warlords, and terrorists. Taken together, these suddenly stronger actors have the power to not only threaten state sovereignty, but also to disrupt the lives, sense of security, and behaviour of individual citizens. In many countries, these problems are so acute that national well-being is being undercut, national priorities are being upended as repressive laws are introduced, and money that was once earmarked for development priorities is now diverted to hiring more police and bodyguards.

Advances in the sciences are likewise problematic. Groundbreaking discoveries have been coupled with serious setbacks and reversals. Diseases, old and new, continue to blight the lives of hundreds of millions. At the end of 2000 roughly 36 million people were living with HIV/AIDS—95 percent were in poor countries.[10] The disease is uprooting social fabrics as countries' citizens are taken away at the prime of their lives and children are left uncared for. In fact, a third of worldwide deaths are attributable to infectious disease caused by bacteria and viruses.[11] Several diseases have developed resistance to traditional antibiotics and vaccine research has been on the decline. And despite the real progress made in the sciences, discoveries often become mired in moral quandaries. Few fields are fraught with more dynamic possibility and moral concern than "stem cell" research. Stem cell research has been condemned by many right-to-life groups despite the ability of researchers to harvest the cells without destroying human embryos. Even though the field holds great promise for curing illness, the complex nature of the debate has caused many concerned governments and would-be funders to withdraw support.

As if the present setbacks posed by globalization were not enough, there is an increasingly loud chorus warning of further calamity. After September 11, 2001, governments are more seriously considering repeated United Nations' warnings over the threat of nuclear terrorism. The Central Intelligence Agency has stated that nuclear technology and the materials to build weapons are "more accessible than at any other time in history" and it is now assumed that a determined terrorist could build an atomic bomb with the necessary fissile materials.[12] Although it is unlikely that terrorists have nuclear technology at this time, there is evidence that groups, including Al Qaeda, have made determined efforts to acquire it.[13]

With the economy expanding at unprecedented rates, there will likely be a parallel expansion in waste and pollution as the environment struggles to keep pace. Irreversible changes in climate, a retreat in social progress, and open warfare are only a few possibilities. Compounded by predictions of an exponential growth in population, the environment and its dependents appear to be in for a rough ride in the years ahead.

New Thinking Needed

With the above in mind, it is not hard to see why many have adopted a pessimistic outlook. Far from saving future generations from the scourge of war, the international community is confronted with a myriad of new threats with no clear solution. Instead of the fresh thinking that is needed, governments are applying outdated logic and solutions to these challenges when innovation is demanded. It is no wonder that the ills of globalization clearly outstrip the benefits. Governments certainly have it within them to create widespread peace, prosperity and justice, but to date they have shown little will to exercise this ability.

As bleak as the prognosis may seem at times, we—as a human family—have a clear choice. Often preoccupied with day-to-day decisions having little individual bearing on the future, collectively, society has little in the way of a determined and well thought-out strategy. The reality is we are entering the future at blinding speed and our very survival hinges on crafting such a strategy. The fact that we still have the luxury of choosing to do so is, in itself, a basis for hope. But, if we continue down our current path, we may someday look back at a time when opportunity slipped away and we lost control of our destiny.

At the same time, we cannot become so confident in our ingenuity that we adopt an air of self-indulgence and triumphalism. Indeed, there is much to be optimistic about: the spread of democracy, successes in science, political achievements, widespread improvements in literacy. There is much to indicate that positive achievement is underway. Indeed, many will reap the rewards. But, as suggested above, this success is—at least in part—based on a selective and myopic view of the available evidence. The dilemmas that do not fit into this optimistic view tend to be downplayed or even downright dismissed.

The terrorists have cruelly drawn our attention to the darker reality of globalization. Unfortunately, the dominant model of international affairs still taught to tomorrow's academics, diplomats and business leaders is grounded in outdated thinking that assumes the sovereign state as the frame of reference. In the immediate wake of September 11, 2001, the hope was that the attacks might shake the foundations of conventional thought and perhaps awaken us from our pessimism and complacency and infuse governments with the will to raise up the public policy discourse. Unfortunately, this has not been the case and each day now brings notice of more guards, controls and surveillance. This misdirected logic is most obvious in the U.S. decision to boost its military spending to nearly $400 billion in fiscal year 2003. Although the biggest military spender, a World Health Organization report ranks the U.S. last in terms of how much of its Gross National Product is spent on foreign aid.[14] This outdated Cold War logic—also evident in the United States' and other countries' approaches to nuclear arms control, the environment, and international law—offers little promise that the world community is adapting well to the new reality. Clearly, a different approach is demanded of us, but we must first adopt an attitude that we can make a difference.

REASONS FOR HOPE

The autonomy once championed by Adam Smith is no longer of much practical use. The fact is, an era defined by global challenges demands global responses. We must realize that the problems and challenges of the future all have a global dimension and that any one country cannot expect to surmount them alone. Instead of relying on technology and power to ensure "national" security, we must instead think in terms of "global" security. This means shifting the resources still being exhausted on old ideas toward creating international mechanisms grounded in dialogue and multilateral cooperation so that the ideals set forth in the United Nations Charter, and reinforced in the Secretary-General's Millennium Report, may prevail. Herein lies the promise of a more hopeful future.

For the first time, our world is sufficiently interdependent and aware of its common challenge that it can—if it chooses—use its collective ingenuity to map out a brighter future. The first option sees a continuation down the present path based on the conviction that technology and market forces are sufficient to bring prosperity and social justice to humankind. But, as argued above, this may necessarily mean a much grimmer future where uneven economic growth creates patches of prosperity interwoven by poverty and despair, growing environmental degradation, conflict, violence and social chaos. The second option is a more optimistic vision of the future where fundamental social, political and economic change can extend security and opportunity to all of humanity.

Such a future, characterized by human ingenuity and compassion, is more than wishful thinking and points to tentative changes already underway that may presage such a transformation. A small but growing number of corporations have come to the conclusion that environmentally sustainable decisions increasingly factor into their profitability and long-term success.[15] For instance, several companies are voluntarily taking initiatives to lessen their environmental impact. Breaking ranks with other energy corporations, the British Petroleum Company has voluntarily supported the need for climate protection. There are also unprecedented working partnerships between such companies and environmental groups including the one between McDonald's Corporation and the Environmental Defense Fund, which has devised innovative ways to recycle plastic containers. Industries such as tobacco, that are not adhering to social expectations, are being put under the microscope and facing increasing difficulty through litigation and regulations. A handful of governments are also attempting to adapt to new realities and are pursuing projects designed to improve their societies. For instance, the Netherlands is endeavouring to transform its entire industrial framework within a generation and provide the basis for long-term quality of life for its citizens.

Although not the dominant trend, these instances demonstrate that forward-thinking and fundamental change are possible. Of course, translating this logic to the global level and having 200 national governments agree what changes need to be made remain gargantuan tasks. Granted, there has been much success in certain areas, including the environment and human rights, but it remains to be seen if such achievement can be extended to more sensitive issues such as disarmament and international justice.

A MAJOR ROLE FOR CIVIL SOCIETY

Civil society has a major role to play in achieving success in these areas. Just as the information revolution has empowered those seeking to harm, it has shown great potential to strengthen those making a positive contribution to disarmament, human rights and development issues. Civil society groups are especially adapted to the dynamics of globalization. While they do not have the military or diplomatic resources of states, they do possess an inherent capability to change shape, to submerge and resurface, and to make decisions rapidly, all important tools of survival in today's world. At the same time, the international organizations that provide the foundation for traditional state-centric diplomacy, in particular the vast United Nations system, can provide conduits for civil society input. Combined with the opportunities presented by the wave of democratization following the end of the Cold War, civil society has been empowered to such an extent that they are now significant actors in their own right.[16] Working together, civil society has joined, but also forged ahead of, governments on an array of issues as disparate as the decommissioning of nuclear reactors, brokering cease-fires in civil wars, and having the World Bank back away from massive dam projects in India, Malaysia, and China.

The information revolution also promises to revolutionize the process of governance and the delivery of public goods. Electronic links between people and between people and their governments can lead to improved social integration, better access to employment opportunities and health services, and more responsive governments. Large strides have been made in this direction in Finland, where Internet access is fast becoming an integral part of the democratic process. Of course, there is much work to be done to ensure that all parts of the world are connected and presented with the same opportunities.

At the same time, more than the latest technology is needed to ensure a better future. Perhaps most important, if we are to navigate today's challenges and leave a legacy of hope for future generations, global awareness and knowledge must be broadened. As evidenced in the campaigns to ban landmines and create an International Criminal Court, there is a direct link between global awareness and institutional change. Of course, technology can be of great assistance in this regard, but it is no substitute for political leadership infused with the prerequisite vision and courage. The ending of apartheid in South Africa and communist rule in Eastern Europe have shown that positive social changes can happen just as rapidly as technological ones.

Global civilization certainly has the power to actively shape its own future and achieve social justice. But having the luxury to choose to use this power will not last indefinitely and a decision cannot be put off much longer. If we continue our current drift toward the future, we may look back and see a time when our creations—both good and bad—overran our ability to control them and we lost control of our destiny. At the same time, trends are not destiny. The forces that underlie current trends are uniquely human processes and outcomes hinge on human hopes and decisions yet to be made.

---

[1] George Herbert Bush, "Address Before a Joint Session of the Congress on the Persian Gulf Crisis and the Federal Budget Deficit," September 11, 1990 (http://bushlibrary.tamu.edu/papers/1990/90091101.html).

2   George Herbert Bush, "Address Before a Joint Session of the Congress on the State of the Union," January 29, 1991 (http://bushlibrary.tamu.edu/papers/1991/91012902.html).

3   George Walker Bush, "State of the Union Address," January 29, 2002 (www.whitehouse.gov).

4   Thomas L. Friedman, *The Lexus and the Olive Tree*, New York: Anchor Books/Random House, 2000, 9.

5   "Profits Over People," *The Economist* – Special Section Surveying Globalization ("Globalization and its Critics"), 29 September 2001, 6.

6   See the *SIPRI Yearbook 2001: Armaments, Disarmament and International Security*, Stockholm International Peace Research Institute, 2001.

7   See "Profits Over People," *The Economist*, 12.

8   United Nations Development Programme (UNDP), *Human Development Report 2001: Making New Technologies Work for Human Development*, New York: Oxford, 2001. Also available on-line at: www.undp.org/hdr2001/completenew.pdf

9   World Resources Institute, *World Resources 1994-95*, (New York: Oxford, 1994), 5.

10 *Human Development Report 2001*, 13.

11 "The Twenty-First Century: Towards the Identification of Some Main Trends," Preliminary Contribution of the Analysis and Forecasting Office to the Work of the Executive Board's Task Force on UNESCO in the Twenty-First Century (4 May 2000), 10.

12 See David Hoffman, "Russia's Nuclear Sieve," *Washington Post*, 17 April 1996, A25, and Bruce G. Blair, "The Ultimate Hatred is Nuclear," *The New York Times*, 22 October 2001, A19.

13 See Kimberly McCloud and Matthew Osborne, "WMD Terrorism and Usama Bin Laden," Center for Nonproliferation Studies. See http://cns.miis.edu/pubs/reports/binladen.htm

14 World Health Organization, "Macroeconomics and Health: Investing in Health for Economic Development," 20 December 2001, http://www3.who.int/whosis/cmh/cmh_report/e/report.cfm

15 See Allen Hammond, *Which World? Scenarios for the 21st Century*, Washington D.C.: Island Press, 1998, 54-61.

16 According to the Union of International Associations in Geneva, the number of international non-governmental organizations has grown from 2,100 in 1972 to roughly 38,000 today. See http://www.uia.org/homeorg.htm

Why There Is Hope for Humanity

By Gene Knudsen Hoffman

W hen I was asked, "Do you have hope for humanity?" my mind said, "No!" My heart said, "Wait a minute. Listen to me." I did. This is what I heard.

I think war and violence are human problems. That's why I'm hopeful. I've seen that humanity can change, and it has—not by force, not by threat, not even by cajoling, but by creating a safe place to be heard, to hear, to accept the other's right to his/her point of view, and to look for truth in it with which we can agree. I believe we all have fragments of truth in our points of view, and it's important we look for those fragments when we're deeply troubled by differences.

We all have secrets, and, it seems to me, secrets are part of our undoing. We hid how cruel the first settlers were to the Indians. These earliest immigrants came here following what I believe were skewed truths about freedom. They believed they had "discovered this land and had a right to it." They believed they had eminent domain over it, the people, the animals, and the vegetation they found here. And they had a right to use them as they chose. Many of us don't believe that any more and are seeking ways to heal this breach.

Many of us felt it was right to own slaves, to keep people in bondage for our use and pleasure, because (we believed) these weren't "real people"—they didn't have souls. Today, many of us believe that was a tragic lie and are seeking ways to heal this breach, too.

We have believed the mountains and seas, animals and trees were "ours" because we found or bought them. Now many of us feel they are the heritage of all of us—and are our caregivers, our friends, and we must cherish them.

We have believed that we had the right to manipulate the earth and its gifts into weapons, to genetically change fruits and vegetables, to clone sheep, clone people, create deadly pesticides, spray them on food, and then, without warning, sell the food for us to eat.

We've long believed that it was our right to declare war against people and topple governments, if not civilizations, when they disagreed with us. We thought we had a God-given right to fight for our "self-interest." We thought it was right to atom-bomb Hiroshima and Nagasaki. Many of us now feel this was wrong, if not disastrous, thinking. Many of us now believe we should continuously be in dialogue, negotiation, mediation, or just plain conversation with those with whom we have ruptured relationships.

The Path of War

And the path of war is the path we still follow today. We are killing people, destroying lands and cities in Afghanistan. We are leaving war's remainders in that land—dead bodies, used weapons, and some weapons which are unfortunately still "alive." We have peopled that country with thousands of military personnel who, no doubt, believe we are ridding the earth of evil with our guns, and our tanks and our bombs. And we are keeping the deadly results secret from ourselves, the public. Instead, we see commercials, which tell us of delightful places we can vacation, basking on beaches in the warm sun, exotic new automobiles to buy, the right cosmetics to make all women beautiful.

Meanwhile, we are told by our president that we are providing "security for our homeland," with a war that will go on and on while we beat a bloody path to "victory over evil."

And now we are readying our weapons of terror to continue this war. We are threatening to take it to countries other than Afghanistan—anywhere people do not agree with our American ideas of freedom and democracy. These wars are spontaneous, unapproved by our Congress. We are terrifying people with our ever-present threat of revenge on those who take revenge on us for past injuries and harm. Through our determination to "destroy evil"—which is an abstraction—we are committing assassinations and making them look respectable. We are on a dangerous path.

"How then," might you ask, "do I have any hope for humanity?"

REVENGE DOES NOT BRING PEACE

My reply: Many of us believe the path we are following leads to disaster. Acting out of revenge does not bring peace—it invariably provokes retaliation in some form. I don't believe we want to live under this threat.

Some of us have learned there are limits to what is allowed us. We have been given freedom, not license. We are being offered lessons we cannot practice until we have a heart that yearns for peace for all. I do not believe we will have ongoing peace until we realize that all life is sacred, and we need to listen to the suffering and grievances of all sides to any conflict.

There are laws we may not disobey without jeopardy to ourselves and all we love, for if we do not honor our limits we enter "chaos and old night." When we fight wars, we are in that chaos. When we harm the earth, we enter chaos. When we do not do our work to heal our wounds—which are a cause of hate, anger, wars, and violence—that chaos is in us.

I believe there is hope for humanity because many of us are relinquishing our secrets and ignorance. Some are moving from denial to acknowledgement of mistakes in our past or present. Some are even asking for forgiveness.

We are learning we cannot make peace if we do not listen to our "enemies" with the same compassion, nonjudgment, and caring we ask for ourselves. Indeed, as Longfellow wrote, "If we could read the secret history of our enemies, we would find sorrow and suffering enough to dispel all hostility."

The Power of Forgiveness

Last, we might reach a depth of understanding that would enable us to ask for forgiveness and forgive—for I do not believe there can ever be real peace without forgiveness. This is hard, because we're not accustomed to admitting that we are wrong.

There are places in the world where people are discovering the need for acknowledging the harm they have done, asking for forgiveness and forgiving. For example, Desmond Tutu, Episcopal Archbishop in South Africa, maintains, "There is no future without forgiveness." Yehezkel Landau, one of the great peacemakers in Israel, writes:

> Diplomats are contriving formulas that might bring Israelis and Palestinians together. The focus, I feel, is missing...is a readiness to admit the harm done to the other side, and to demonstrate repentance for that behavior. This is a challenge diplomacy tends to ignore—this may be why all [peacework] in the Middle East comes to naught.

> The hardest and most essential sacrifice required for genuine peace is that of one's self-image as the innocent victim at the hands of a cruel enemy. Imagine how cathartic it might be if [Israeli] public figures said words like these:

> "In defending ourselves, we projected on you demonic stereotypes.... The violence you waged against unarmed Jews caused us great pain and anger.... Yet we hope you can forgive our violence against you and ... for so many of you in exile from the land. Now, let us together transform this legacy into a hopeful future by agreeing to partition land into two states for two peoples who claim it."

> Israelis need to hear similar words from Palestinians such as:

> "We Palestinians were the majority in Palestine when European Jews began settling the land—this meant the loss of our land and our political rights to people who weren't born here. Looking back with greater compassion, we can forgive you... for the same nationalist excesses that we, too, have been guilty of. Let us transcend the antagonism of the past, affirm our recognition of one another, and accept the rights and needs of both sides."

Desmond Tutu, one of the founders of the Truth and Reconciliation Commission in South Africa, maintains, "...on the foundation of forgiveness can be built the transformation of conflicts. Forgiveness-based negotiations start with the premise that conflict leads to death. Not merely physical death, but the death of trust, the termination of relationships, the sowing of deadly hatred."

FORGIVENESS IN ACTION

What might happen if some of us followed the lead of remarkable men such as Desmond Tutu? What if we began making pilgrimages in little groups to places where we have harmed people through war? What if we went to Japan to acknowledge the horrors that our atom bombs unleashed upon the Japanese, and asked for forgiveness? What if we went to Korea, Vietnam, Graneda, Cuba, Nicaragua, El Salvador, Iraq, and Afghanistan to speak our sorrow for the destruction we caused them? What if we offered to make personal restitution and asked for forgiveness?

Might such actions lead to the transformation of humanity that some of us feel is necessary if life is to continue on earth? I think they would, and it could be a proof that a small group of dedicated people can make mighty changes. I think true reconciliation, mutual healing, mutual understanding, mutual love might spring up between strangers who were once enemies. And it might mean the continuation of a healthier planet and a noble human race.

"To Be Human or Not to Be" Is Today's Choice

BY FREDERICK FRANCK

W hat it means to be Human is the question that has dominated my inner life from my fifth year until now, at over
ninety. I have written a few books about it to clarify it maximally in
my mind. And so when someone questioned me the other day:
"How can we become more Human?" I answered at once: "By being less beastly," for when we sink below the human level, we do
not become sub-human, but sub-animal! And it is this fateful re-
gression I must have become aware of when, as a five-year-old,
born on the Dutch-Belgian border, I saw the twentieth century begin in earnest on August 4, 1914.

The Kaiser's armies invaded Belgium half a mile from our door-
step. The First World War had started. The big German field guns
were booming all too close by, and almost at once an endless stream
of wounded and dying soldiers on improvised ambulances, push-
carts, and horse-drawn wagons crossed the border into neutral
Holland. Endless files of wretched humans, fleeing their burning
villages, passed my window, children and belongings on their
backs—advance guard of the millions of uprooted ones who would
trudge from border to border all through this tragic century.

I happened to survive the twentieth century almost from beginning to end. I even outlived—sheer miracle—its blood-thirsty de-
mons: Kaiser Wilhelm, Franco, Hitler, Stalin, and their heinous ilk;
their monstrous wars, gulags, extermination camps; their massa-

cres, genocides, mass murders; all their unforgivable sins against the Spirit.

And so it could happen that, in the spring of 1995, the year of the nightmares of Rwanda, East Timor, Tibet, and Srebenica raging in unabated fury, we met in a coffee shop in Greenwich Village, talking about that much touted new millennium just around the corner, that third millennium after Golgotha. What was going to be so "new," starting on January 1, 2000? Didn't it look more likely to be nothing but a replay of the frightful millennium limping to its close, perhaps its terminal replay?

The new millennium that started two years ago announced itself convincingly, all too frightfully, on September 11, 2001. We wondered, is there nothing to be done, nothing at all? Are we doomed, are we condemning ourselves to slide passively into that terminal barbarity? And who are "we," gathered here: a baker's dozen of New Yorkers—a few artists, a clergyman, a lawyer, a TV producer, a biologist couple, a nun, a musician, a physicist... poor mortals all, self-appointed representatives of humanity. Was it all hopeless? Was the real "we"—humanity—really done for?

CONTEMPT FOR LIFE

"Look," said one of us suddenly, "the very fact that we are sitting here, mulling over our predicament, couldn't that mean there is still a glimpse of hope? For surely we are not the only ones whose spiritual immune systems have not broken down completely. We are not so special! And if we are not so special, it means there must be millions like us, still unaffected by this rabies of the soul, this virus of *contempt for life*. No, we are not alone!"

"I couldn't agree more," I said, "for I run into them wherever I go, all over this country, Europe, Japan. I meet them where least expected. They are ordinary people as we are, who—against all odds— seem still unestranged from their basic human sanity, their capacities for insight, empathy, compassion, and who have not yet given up on what is human in us humans. The trouble is that they sit isolated on their little islands, incommunicado, either alone or in little clusters, as we are sitting here, out of contact with the many out there!"

"If that is so," the musician said, "and no doubt it is, we belong to something that could be a powerful antidote to the cynicism and *contempt for life*, however unorganized, even unorganizable, it may be. So it is actually a matter of establishing real contact, communication among the islanders, and that is tough enough, but it is possible!

"Now, let us imagine that we, around this table, are a core with the formidable task of establishing contact, nay, communication among those millions of islanders. We'd have to realize that such a contact would have to crystallize around something very simple, very basic, to counteract this virus of *contempt for life* in our time, this obsession with death and with the tools of death that pervade the world."

REVERENCE FOR LIFE

The words *contempt for life* had fallen again, and made me think at once of *Reverence for Life*, Albert Schweitzer's life motto, which he lived from 1915 to his death in 1965: "*Reverence for Life* is the one principle on which a viable ethic can be founded," he wrote.

I saw him apply it in practice while serving on his medical staff in Lambarene from 1958 to 1961. *Reverence for Life* was the guiding principle in everything he did. It was free from sentimentality. It was simply the avoidance of inflicting unnecessary suffering on any living being, and the alleviation of suffering with all the medical and human means at his disposal. *Reverence for Life* was for him the basis, not only of an ethic, but also of all truly human relationships with our fellow humans and with all that lives.

I was drawing the old man, he was eighty-six then, as he sat writing at his desk, his face almost touching the paper, his bristling mustache at times sweeping it as the old hand wrote on, slowly, painstakingly. Once in a while his head would straighten to turn toward the screened window that looked out over the river. Turning back, for an instant aware of me, he mumbled a few words and went on writing. It was getting dark. The file of his pet ants marching across the paper went out of focus in the falling dusk. He stopped his writing, got up stiffly, put on his faded, crumpled felt hat, and said, "Let's sit outside."

We sat on the steps of his cabin, mutely watching the dusk deepening on the Ogowe River. He looked worried. "One should have the skin of a hippo," he suddenly grunted without explanation, "and the soul of an angel." His little mongrel, Tzu-Tzu, sat contentedly between us. "Ah! Look at that tree," he said after a while, pointing at a kapok tree in the distance, still gleaming in the setting sun. Then all of a sudden—it sounded at once hopeless and hopeful— "Do you think that the idea of *Reverence for Life* is really gaining ground?"

I was perplexed. I felt my eyes getting moist. I had just flown across half of a world that seemed to be getting ready to destroy itself in a spasm of violence. What could I say? "Who knows?"

I tried, "there is such terrible violence all over, isn't there? Still, you sowed the seed. If anyone did, you did sow the seed."

He sighed, "*Ja, ja,*" and got up, for the dinner bell was ringing.

This happened almost forty years ago, and I am older now than Schweitzer was then. What else is it but *Reverence for Life* that motivated the great prophets of human solidarity in the cruel pandemonium of the past century: Gandhi, Bonhoeffer, Martin Luther King, Yehudi Menuhin, Elie Wiesel, Daisetz Teitaro Suzuki; and, for me (non-affiliated *homo religiosus*) no one more than that genius of the heart, Pope John XXIII—among countless anonymous men and women in all parts of the world. What they really have in common must be a freedom from all cynicism, a love of humans, a love of life, and a passionate awe for the Ultimate Mystery called "life."

"Don't you idealize Schweitzer?" I was asked. "He has been accused of being a paternalist, even a racist." I replied that I didn't idealize him. He was the product of the colonial era, but literally day and night, for fifty years, he brought medical help where none was available, and he wrote: "Our task is to do everything possible to protect the human rights of the Africans we have forced to assume the burden of a foreign, technological culture." Schweitzer was not just a pioneer of human rights, he was also a pioneer in foreign aid—without any political or ideological strings attached—

and as a missionary he did not convert anyone, did not preach Christian love but simply practiced it. At the same time he was a pioneer in practical ecumenism. I heard him stop short a *Time* reporter, who started to theologize, with "Dogma divides, the Spirit unites." And finally, when Schweitzer was deep in his eighties, he was once more the pioneer—the first public figure of his stature—to protest vigorously against nuclear testing. "We are constantly being told about permissible amounts of radiation. Who permits it? Who has the right to permit it?" he wrote.

Reverence for Life implies the insight, the empathy and compassion that mark the maturation of the human inner process. That maturation implies overcoming the split between thinking and feeling that is the bane of our scientism and our idolization of technology that distances—estranges—us from all emotional and ethical constraints. This same distancing, this objectification of the unobjectifiable, is characteristic of racism, ethnic cleansing, cruelty, and exploitation of the other by political, racial, religious collectivized in-group egos, including that global free-market mentality for which all that is, is looked upon as mere raw material-for-profit, even if it ruins our species and our earth forever.

Suddenly we seemed invaded by those millions from their isolated little islands, urging us to risk a preliminary attempt at inter-island communication.

No, we are not drifting away from our formidable task of linking the isolated little islands of sanity and humanness. *Reverence for Life* versus *Contempt for Life* might well be that single, simple crystallization point all can share.

"Are you aware," the biologist asked, "that what we are at the point of embarking on is a very risky experiment? It invites being shrugged off as pitifully naïve, ridiculed as paranoid, megalomaniac, or whatever."

YOU ARE NOT ALONE!

But one thing we agreed upon: There is no point at all in starting yet another prestigious and expensive symposium. All we could do, we concluded, was to put ourselves on the line, and so we each committed ourselves to writing directly from the heart on what we consider essential, on the criteria of being human or less than human at this *technotronic* juncture. We would write it as it came, naturally, freely, out of our own life experience, in our own language, with as few prestigious quotes as possible. Apart from writing this personal credo in one or a few pages, we each undertook to prevail on at least two others we knew to do likewise. Once we had gathered a few dozen of these intimate, personal communications—however varied in tone—we would study them as to their relevance to our shared human condition in this fateful era and decide whether our harvest merited publication. It would be a book that could function as a living link with our counterparts on their little islands, if only to reassure and encourage them: You are not alone! You are not mad! There are millions of us!

Not only did each of us write that brief paper and inspire others to do the same, but within a few months we had gathered many more responses than we had hoped for. The experiment had turned itself into a chain reaction in which the *Vox Humana* was clearly audible.

And so a book, *What does it mean to be Human? Reverence for Life Reaffirmed*, was published by St. Martin's Press in the year 2000. Contributors included 100 respondents from all walks of life, including six Nobel Prize Laureates: the Dalai Lama, Archbishop Tutu, Elie Wiesel, Joseph Rotblat, Mother Teresa, Oscar Arias, the great violinist Yehudi Menuhin, and authors like Huston Smith, Thomas Berry, Nancy Willard, Vaclav Havel, Joanna Macy, Satish Kumar, Virginia Mollenkott, Rustum Roy, Anne Wilson-Schaef, James Earl Jones, Daniel Berrigan, David Krieger, and many others.

And so the publication of this chain reaction does not aspire to be either entertaining or literary gourmet fare, but intends only to be a timely documentation of resistance to the slide into post-human barbarism in this age of nuclear menace. It is a sign of hope for the possibility of reestablishing, against all odds, the heart-to-heart contact that bridges our isolation—indeed an act of faith in the survival of our species as a human species.

hope
FINDING THE WAY

Hope in the Face of Darkness

By David Krieger

E ach life is a miracle. Each of us is a miracle. We cannot explain by logic or experience where we come from before birth or where we go after death. We have no way to comprehend the mystery of life or the mystery of our universe. We can only appreciate that we exist on this Earth at this time in this vast and expanding universe, and try to use our precious lives for good purposes.

As shocking as terrorism may be, it is far from our only problem or even our major problem. We still live in a world in which thousands of children die daily from starvation and preventable diseases.

We live in a world in which the richest 20 percent control 80 percent of the resources. Some 500 billionaires own combined wealth equal to that owned by over half of the world's population. While some on our planet live in lavish abundance, with every material advantage imaginable, others live in abject poverty, lacking even the basic resources needed to survive.

The world spends $850 billion annually on military forces and weapons, while for a fraction of this amount everyone on the planet could have clean water, adequate food, health care, education, shelter, and clothing.

There are 30 to 40 wars going on at any given time. Greed, lust for power, injustice, disparity, and old and new hatreds give rise to these wars. The vast majority of the casualties are civilians. In these wars, some 300,000 child soldiers participate. These wars destroy the environment and the infrastructure in already poor countries, and produce new masses of refugees.

In many parts of the world, people suffer from massive human rights abuses. These abuses fall most heavily on women and children.

As a species, but particularly in the so-called developed world, we are using up the resources of our planet at a prodigious rate. In doing so, we are robbing future generations of their ability to share in the use of these resources.

We are also polluting our land, air and water—our most precious resources that we need for survival—with chemical, biological and radiological poisons.

If all of this were not enough, we have developed and deployed tens of thousands of nuclear weapons capable of destroying humanity and most of life. Many people think that this problem has ended, but it has not. There are still more than 30,000 nuclear weapons in the world, and some 4,500 of them are on hair-trigger alert.

WE SHOULD ALL BE CONCERNED

We have reached a point where all of us should be concerned and responsive. Things could grow still worse, however. Nuclear, chemical, or biological weapons in the hands of terrorists would multiply the dangers. Instead of buildings being destroyed, nuclear weapons could cause the destruction of whole cities. Imagine the damage that could be done if terrorists had nuclear weapons. This danger cannot be dismissed.

Humanity can no longer afford or tolerate the damage that hatred can cause. Nor can humanity afford or tolerate the suffering and premature death that has been the lot of the poor.

Far too many people on this Earth live in despair and hopelessness. These are afflictions of the soul that go beyond physical pain. Others, who should know better, live in selfishness, ignorance, and apathy. In many ways, these are even crueler afflictions of the soul.

It is not always easy to have hope in the face of darkness, but it is necessary. If we give up hope for bringing about change, we give away our power and diminish the possibilities for change.

Hope must be a conscious choice. There are always reasons for giving up and retreating into selfishness, ignorance and apathy. If you want change, you must choose hope. It will not necessarily choose you. The way to choose hope is by your actions to achieve a better world.

THE POWER OF THE HUMAN SPIRIT

There are important reasons to have hope. The most important reason for me is the power of the human spirit. The human spirit is capable of achieving sublime beauty and overcoming tremendous obstacles. All greatness—in art, music, literature, science, engineering, and peace—is a triumph of the human spirit. But the greatest triumph of the human spirit comes from choosing a compassionate goal and persisting in overcoming obstacles to achieve this goal. All worthy goals require persistence to achieve. They will not happen overnight.

We should celebrate the spirit of the *hibakusha*, the survivors of the atomic bombings of Hiroshima and Nagasaki at the end of World War II. They are still fighting for a better world, a world in which nuclear weapons will never again be used. They have been proposed to receive the Nobel Prize for Peace. I would strongly support their nomination for this recognition and high honor.

Miyoko Matsubara was a young girl when the bomb was dropped on Hiroshima. She has had a dozen or more surgeries and has suffered from breast cancer, but her spirit is indomitable. She learned English and has traveled throughout the United States and Europe to tell her story to young people in the hope that they will understand nuclear dangers and not suffer her fate. When I think of Miyoko, I think of her humble but determined spirit. She is a woman who has suffered and who bows deeply.

Sadako Sasaki was two years old when the bomb fell on Hiroshima. When she was 12 years old she suffered from leukemia as a result of her exposure to radiation, and was hospitalized. Wishing to be healthy again, she folded paper cranes. She folded some two-thirds of the 1000 paper cranes that she hoped would make her wish come true. On one of these paper cranes she wrote, "I will write peace on your wings and you will fly all over the world."

After Sadako died, her classmates finished folding the cranes. Today Sadako's statue stands in Hiroshima Peace Memorial Park. Nearby the statue are thousands of strands of paper cranes that have been brought there by children from throughout Japan and from throughout the world. Children all over the world know of Sadako's story and her courage.

Nelson Mandela fought for the rights of his people and an end to apartheid in South Africa. The government of South Africa put him in prison, where he remained for 27 years. Despite his imprisonment, he was able to maintain his spirit and his hope. When he was finally released from prison, he became the first black president of his country. Instead of seeking vengeance, he presided over a peaceful transition of power in South Africa, appointing a Truth and Reconciliation Commission to offer pardons to all who confessed their crimes and misdeeds during the period of apartheid.

There are so many people whose lives reflect the best of the human spirit. Another is Hafsat Abiola, who was one of the Nuclear Age Peace Foundation's honorees for our 2001 Distinguished Peace Leadership Award. Hafsat's father was the first democratically elected president of Nigeria, but he was not able to serve even one day because he was imprisoned by the military. When Hafsat's mother fought for democracy in her country and for her husband's release from prison, she was assassinated. On the day before Hafsat's father was to be released from prison, he, too, was killed.

Despite the pain of losing her parents, Hafsat is without bitterness or rancor. After graduating from Harvard University, she started an organization named for her mother, the Kudirat Initiative for Democracy (KIND). Hafsat works for democracy and for the rights of women and children throughout Africa.

Another of many examples of the power of the human spirit is found in Nobel Peace Laureate Mairead Corrigan Maguire. Mairead was a young woman working as a secretary in Northern Ireland when disaster struck her family. Mairead's sister and her sister's three young children were hit by an out-of-control car when British forces shot an IRA getaway driver. All three of the children died, and the pain was so great that Mairead's sister later committed suicide.

Mairead debated what she should do. She considered taking up arms against the British, but she instead choose the course of non-violence. Mairead and another woman, Betty Williams, organized peace gatherings in Northern Ireland. They brought together hundreds of thousands of ordinary people calling for peace. The important thing to note is that Mairead herself was a very ordinary person, who became extraordinary because of the courage, compassion and commitment of her choices. Today she is the most active of the Nobel Peace Laureates, and often brings them together to speak and act on important peace issues.

Even Improbable Change Does Occur

A second reason for hope is that even improbable change does occur. Changes that no expert could predict sometimes occur with incredible speed. Relationships change and new possibilities for peace open up, such as occurred in US-China relations in the early 1970s. The Cold War ended after more than four decades of tension and conflict between East and West. This was symbolized by the fall of the Berlin Wall, which opened the way for a reunited Germany. Pieces of that wall with their graffiti are now souvenirs sold to tourists. I have a small piece of the wall in my office. It reminds me that even great barriers can come down.

Nelson Mandela went from being a prisoner of a repressive government to becoming president of South Africa. Similar stories mark the lives of Lech Walesa of Poland and Vaclav Havel of the Czech Republic. These changes are not predictable, and are usually the result of efforts that have been taking place over a long period of time by committed individuals, generally outside the glare of the media spotlight.

The Power of One

A third reason for hope is the Power of One. Individuals can and do make a difference in our world. The second person our Foundation honored with our 2001 Distinguished Peace Leadership Award was Craig Kielburger. Craig was only 18 years old when we honored him, but he was already an old hand at social change. What changed Craig's life was reading about a 12-year-old Pakistani boy, Iqbal Masih, when Craig was himself only 12 years old. Iqbal had been sold into bonded labor as a carpet weaver and had been virtually a slave, chained to his carpet loom for 14 to 16 hours a day. Somehow he had been able to get free, and began speaking out against child labor. Iqbal was given the Reebok Human Rights Award, but when he returned to Pakistan he was murdered by the "Carpet mafia."

Craig thought about Iqbal being the same age as he was. When Craig went to school that day, he told his friends about Iqbal and insisted that they do something to further the cause of children's rights for which Iqbal had been fighting. That was the beginning of a new organization, Kids Can Free the Children, founded by Craig Kielburger at the age of 12.

Today, Craig's organization has grown to over 100,000 members. It is the largest organization of children helping children in the world. Kids Can Free the Children has been responsible for freeing thousands of children from bonded labor, and they have built hundreds of schools in places where children were previously not able to obtain a basic education. Craig travels throughout the world to learn and to inspire young people to get involved and make a difference.

To reiterate, three important reasons to have hope are: the power of the human spirit; the fact that improbable change does occur; and the Power of One. The most important reason, though, is that hope is needed to change the world, and you cannot leave this job to others. Your hope and your help are needed.

The Enemies of Hope

The greatest enemies of change are selfishness, apathy and ignorance. These also are the enemies of hope. I urge you to resist these at all costs.

Selfishness is a narrow way to live. It is about what you have and keep to yourself, not about what you do. Rich lives are not about the money we accumulate, but about the ways in which we interconnect and help others. *The antidote to selfishness is compassion, built upon helping others.*

Apathy is about not caring. It is a lack of interest in others and a failure to engage in trying to make a difference. *The antidote to apathy is caring and commitment.*

Ignorance in the midst of information is also about not caring—not caring enough to find out about the problems that confront us. I recently visited Sadako Peace Garden, the small garden that we created in Santa Barbara on the fiftieth anniversary of the bombing of Hiroshima. Each year on August 6th we hold a commemoration at the garden for all who died and suffered in Hiroshima and Nagasaki.

It is a very beautiful natural garden, with many wonderful trees, including one immense and dramatic eucalyptus tree at one end of the garden called the Tree of Faith. The garden also has large rocks in which cranes have been carved in remembrance of Sadako.

In that garden, people sometimes leave folded paper cranes and short messages hanging from the oak trees. On the day I visited, I found this message: "There are many things here I do not know, the knowing of which could change everything." What a powerful message. *The antidote to ignorance is knowledge.*

We must be seekers of knowledge, not for its own sake but to better understand our world so that we can engage in it and break our bonds of selfishness with a compassionate response to life. I don't think this is asking too much of ourselves or each other. It is the essence of being human.

Don't be constrained by national boundaries. Recognize the

essential equality and dignity of every person on the planet. This is the basic starting point of the Universal Declaration of Human Rights.

Don't expect to change the world overnight. Change seldom occurs that way. Trees grow from seeds. They all begin small, and some grow large. Sometimes they become magnificent. Often they need care and nurturing. Most of what we do to achieve a better world will require patience and persistence.

Plant the Seeds of Peace

I encourage you to plant seeds of peace by your engagement in issues of social justice, by your efforts to create a more decent world in which everyone can live with dignity.

I carry with me a seed from the Tree of Faith in Sadako Peace Garden. It has within it all that is necessary to become a great magnificent tree, just as you have within you all that is needed to become a great human being and a leader for peace.

I want to conclude by asking you to take three specific actions.

First, take the pledge of Earth Citizenship: "I pledge allegiance to the Earth and to its varied life forms; one World, indivisible, with liberty, justice and dignity for all." That is the world we need to create. I also want to encourage you to study two very important documents, *The Universal Declaration of Human Rights* and the *Earth Charter*. Be an active and responsible citizen of our planet. Nothing less will do.

Second, help to build schools in areas of great need. Join with Kids Can Free the Children to raise funds to build schools in post-conflict areas, such as Chiapas, Mexico and Sierra Leone in Africa. For between $5,000 and $10,000 a school can be built and a teacher provided for students who would otherwise not get a primary education. Kids Can Free the Children has already built over 100 of these schools in poor countries. This is one of the best ways I can think of to make a difference in our world.

Third, make a commitment to work for a nuclear weapons-free future. Recognize the essential truth that human beings and nuclear weapons cannot co-exist. Choose peace and a human future. Work to make your school, your community, your nation, and our world nuclear weapons-free zones. Organize letter writing and petition campaigns to the media and to government leaders. Promote the idea of a Nobel Peace Prize for the *hibakusha* of Hiroshima and Nagasaki to bring global attention to their plea of "Never Again!" Use the sunflower as the symbol of achieving a nuclear weapons-free world.

I urge you also to join us in gathering support for the Nuclear Age Peace Foundation's Appeal to End the Nuclear Weapons Threat to Humanity and All Life, and sending it to leaders of your country and other countries throughout the world. The Appeal, which has already been signed by some of the great peace leaders of our time, asks the leaders of the nuclear weapons states to take five critical actions for the benefit of all humanity. These are:

- De-alert all nuclear weapons and de-couple all nuclear warheads from their delivery vehicles.

- Reaffirm commitments to the 1972 Anti-Ballistic Missile Treaty and ratify the Comprehensive Test Ban Treaty.

- Commence good faith negotiations to achieve a Nuclear Weapons Convention requiring the phased elimination of all nuclear weapons, with provisions for effective verification and enforcement.

- Declare policies of No First Use of nuclear weapons against other nuclear weapons states and policies of No Use against non-nuclear weapons states.

- Reallocate resources from the tens of billions of dollars currently being spent for maintaining nuclear arsenals to improving human health, education, and welfare throughout the world.

Not one of these critical actions was even addressed by Presidents Bush and Putin at their summit in Crawford, Texas in November, 2001. Their treaty to reduce their arsenals of strategic nuclear weapons to between 2,200 and 1,700 over a ten-year period is inadequate and represents their desire to continue to rely upon their nuclear arsenals. We must ask that these leaders return to the negotiating table to take up again the issue of nuclear disarmament in a far more serious way. If they do not, they and we will face the risk that terrorists will be able to purchase, steal, or develop nuclear weapons and destroy our cities.

I would encourage delegations of youth representatives to travel to Washington, Moscow, London and other key capitals to make the case for ending the nuclear weapons threat to humanity and all life. We cannot rely upon the leaders of the nuclear weapons states to solve the problems themselves. They need the help and encouragement of all of us. This is part of our responsibility as citizens of planet Earth.

If serious progress on nuclear disarmament is not made soon, today's youth will be inheriting the nuclear dangers that are left behind. Time is of the essence and we must approach nuclear disarmament now, as if the future of civilization depended upon our success in convincing world leaders to adequately control and eliminate these weapons and the fissile materials needed to create them.

I hope that I have challenged you, particularly with the actions I have proposed. I have confidence that you will meet the challenge of being an active participant in creating a more just and decent future for humanity, a future you can be proud to pass on to your children and grandchildren.

I encourage you to choose hope and then never lose hope, even in the face of darkness. Your success in life will be something that only you can judge, but I believe the right criteria for you to use are compassion, commitment, and courage. I hope that you will work to achieve a better world, and I know that you can and will make a difference.

The Deep Bow of a Hibakusha

for Miyoko Matsubara

She bowed deeply. She bowed deeper than the oceans. She bowed form the top of Mt. Fuji to the bottom of the ocean. She bowed so deeply and so often that the winds blew hard.

The winds blew her whispered apologies and prayers across all the continents. But the winds whistled too loudly, and made it impossible to hear her apologies and prayers. The winds made the oceans crazy. The water in the oceans rose up in a wild molecular dance. The oceans threw themselves against the continents. The people were frightened. They ran screaming from the shores. They feared the white water and the whistling wind. They huddled together in dark places. They strained to hear the words in the wind.

In some places there were some people who thought they heard an apology. In other places there were people who thought they heard a prayer.

She bowed deeply. She bowed more deeply than anyone should bow.

—David Krieger

61

An Evolutionary Perspective

BY BARBARA MARX HUBBARD

My hope for humanity's future springs from the new understanding of the process of evolution, the story of cosmogenesis. Through cosmogenesis, we discover that for 15 billion years our universe has been evolving, and continues to evolve, toward higher consciousness and greater freedom through more complex order, from sub-atomic particles to human beings—us. When we place ourselves into that awesome continuum of transformation, we realize that as humanity, we are yearning to evolve in the same direction. Our higher values, impulses, and aspirations are not just wishful thinking against the apparently implacable force of current reality and entropy, but are actually expressions of the universe within pressing us to evolve to our next stage of being through "syntropy," the fundamental tendency in nature to realize dormant potentials and to self-transcend.

From this evolutionary perspective, we notice that we happen to be living through a period of quantum transformation, a huge jump from one stage of evolution to the next.

Through our expanded understanding of nature from scientific and technological advances, we have gained powers we at one time attributed only to our gods. Now, we can destroy our world or we can cocreate an immeasurable future. The time frame for this change is short. We have learned, quite suddenly, that within the next 10 to 20 years we could irreversibly damage our planetary life support systems to result in our own extinction.

Such a point has been described by Ervin Laszlo as a "macroshift, a bifurcation in the evolutionary dynamics of a society—in our interacting and interdependent world, it is a bifurcation of human civilization in its quasi totality. . . . The chaotic state is not an unordered, random state but one where even immeasurably small fluctuations produce measurable, macroscopic effects. . . . When a human society reaches the limits of its stability, it becomes supersensitive and is highly responsive to the smallest fluctuation."[1]

While evolution normally occurs through incremental change over long periods, at the time of bifurcations, the process speeds up and occurs quickly. If we are living through such a shift, we can expect radical change, even in our lifetime. It is also true at such times of bifurcations that small islands of coherence can have a much greater effect than usual. Therefore, those of us who are participating in conscious positive change can expect to be more effective than times of linear, incremental change would allow.

FROM UNCONSCIOUS TO CONSCIOUS EVOLUTION

Because of our increasing power, we are forced to become conscious of the effect we have on our own evolution, and to participate in guiding that evolutionary process toward ethical ends—or devolve and possibly become extinct.

We are literally experiencing the evolution of evolution itself, from unconscious to conscious evolution.

But why would we assume that all this is possible? Hasn't everything always been like it is? No, of course it hasn't. Look back a couple of hundred thousand years—no *Homo sapiens*.[2] Look back a billion years—no biosphere. Look further back, four and a half-billion years ago—no Earth!

Here is the *new* good news. From the evolutionary perspective, we can see that nature has been taking such quantum jumps as we are now experiencing for billions of years, that it is the nature of nature to transform. From pre-life came life, from animals humans evolved. Now the question is: What may come from us, or indeed, what *is* coming? For the radically new situation now is not quantum change, but the fact that we are the first species on planet Earth to be conscious of participating in such a change, and therefore are possibly able to guide our actions accordingly. This is a stunning opportunity for the big-brained creature, possibly the unexpected key to unlock the capacities and consciousness required for our own quantum transformation.

The most important basis of hope is, I believe, that we are not doing this alone, in a neutral universe. Whatever process, tendency, implicate order, generating force, or Spirit brought existence from sub-atomic particles to the present is still operating through us now. Not only may "the force be with us," but it is also *within* us.

At the root of this view, evolution is not seen as a mechanical, accidental process, nor as a process controlled by an external deity, but as a "living universe,"[3] an awesomely intelligent expression of universal consciousness pervading all being, now rising to self-awareness in the human species. We are the universe becoming conscious of itself. As Pir Vilayat Khan says, *"We are learning to think like the universe."*[4]

The higher forms of life that we are moving toward are not predetermined, but are pre-potential, awaiting our choice to be actualized. The future is a contingency, not an inevitability. We are becoming co-authors of our own destiny.

Each of the world's great faiths has had its own evolutionary exponent to guide its individual tradition, for example, Teilhard de Chardin for Catholicism,[5] Sri Aurobindo for Hinduism and Vedanta,[6] and Pir Vilayat Khan (a Sufi) for Islam.[7]

We also find that many contemporary evolutionary theorists and systems scientists are bridging the divide between science and spirit, seeking the deeper patterns of nature that lead to higher forms of order and consciousness. These include Bela H. Banathy;[8] Peter Russell;[9] Duane Elgin;[10] Brian Swimme;[11] Christopher Bache;[12] Elisabet Sahtouris;[13] Ervin Laszlo;[14, 15, 16], Jean Houston;[17] Riane Eisler;[18] Beatrice Bruteau,[19] and many others.

Given this evolutionary perspective, let's see how several lessons of our evolutionary past can provide guidelines for us now, and how our very problems may be key factors in providing hope for humanity's future.

THREE LESSONS OF EVOLUTION

Lesson Number One: As systems become more complex, they tend to jump towards consciousness and freedom.

From atoms to molecules to cells to animals and humans, and now to humanity going around the next turn on the great evolutionary spiral, there has been a rise in awareness and in freedom through more synergistic and complex order. This pattern is occurring again in our generation. It is clear that planet Earth is complexifying. Our environments, our cultures, our communication and defense systems are rapidly interconnecting—whether we like one another or not! Through the electronic media, especially the Internet, we are becoming one living system. The pain of one has become the pain of all.

We can see, in fact, that millions of us are developing a more empathic consciousness as we become more aware of the suffering which extends beyond our own families and tribes. We seek to preserve other species and the web of nature. We are developing a "whole-system," or a planetary, consciousness. Although this expanded awareness is not yet in dominion in existing social structures, such as the nation-state or the corporation, it is nonetheless emergent. We are learning to be coevolutionary with nature, to understand natural systems and to develop in harmony with them. We are seeking to design new social systems that are synergistic and in alignment with both natural systems and the human spirit, as in the work of Dee Hock.[20] When we look back at the emergence of life out of pre-life, or humans out of animals, we develop "evolutionary eyes," and begin to notice and support emergent properties—new capacities and consciousness rising among us now.

Lesson Number Two: Holism is inherent in the nature of reality. Nature forms new whole systems out of separate parts.

Nature takes jumps through greater synergy. During conditions of disequilibrium, there is a tendency in nature for novel interactions to speed up and converge. Right now we can see that our global system is out of balance—the gap between the rich and poor is widening, the global economic system is unjust and unstable, environmental degradation continues. This cannot go on indefinitely. As we said before, the time frame for changing our behavior is short. Slow, incremental change over hundreds of years will not suffice. There must be a way to foster non-linear, exponential change, and I believe there is. It is to increase synergy and cooperation among creative and loving initiatives.

When we look with evolutionary eyes, we see breakdowns in the old system everywhere, and concurrently, breakthroughs cropping up, innovations and projects that lead to the healing and evolving of our world, such as a growing emphasis on personal and spiritual development, new sources of energy, new alternative health care, holistic education, partnership models in human relations, and organizational transformation. Groups and projects of all kinds are addressing every possible situation in the effort to make a better world.

Increasing connection among the many innovations now can help the system repattern to more complex and harmonious order, following in the great 15-billion-year tradition of quantum transformation. When we connect these breakthroughs, we can see and consciously foster the new culture emerging in our midst.

Lesson Number Three: Problems are evolutionary drivers.

Let's look briefly at the effect on the future of humanity of our two most dangerous problems: the environmental crisis and the threat of nuclear war.

The Environmental Crisis. The human species is being forced for its very survival to grow up, to evolve. We are learning that we are related and connected to all life, and so are responsible for our larger planetary body and for one another. If global warming increases, if the ozone layer continues to thin, if the soil, the seas, and the air are further polluted, we may experience irreversible damage to our life-support systems. Rich and poor alike will suffer.

The old adage of "love your neighbor as yourself" is becoming an operational necessity. Even though there is a terrible widening gap right now between the rich and the poor, ultimately we are all members of this one living system. *There is a built-in limit to greed.* We *must* understand how natural systems work so that we can work naturally with them. We have to align human values with the larger natural systems, and become consciously coevolutionary with nature or become extinct.

Can you imagine what this will mean if we succeed? It means that we will have evolved in consciousness from our self-conscious stage to a more whole-system, planetary, and then universal stage of consciousness. What the mystics experienced—that we are one, interrelated whole—is becoming a functional requirement for survival.

It is the nature of nature to transcend when it hits limits. We will discover that our own yearning for transcendence and transformation is not a mere longing, but in fact the very tendency of the great creating process within us, pressing us to a higher level of consciousness and capacity. We will reinforce our own tendency to transform personally, socially, and technologically in harmony with the patterns of nature. The effect of this potential is unknown.

The Nuclear Crisis. When Einstein revealed to us the formula $E=mc^2$, the necessity for species evolution was triggered. The human mind had penetrated into one of nature's invisible technologies of creation, the atom. Into the hands of a still self-centered humanity came the power to destroy our world. We made the bomb. Now there are enough nuclear weapons to destroy ourselves many times over. It is becoming clear to millions that we must learn to go beyond war as a means of conflict resolution. If we were to use this ultimate weapon in an all-out war, we would experience a nuclear winter, a destruction of ourselves and of all life on earth.

Although the response is slow, as it is to the environmental crisis, and we seem to be going in the opposite direction for the moment, there is nonetheless a built-in limit to violence at the nuclear level. We will either learn to cooperate or we will self-destruct. The nuclear threat already is forcing the human species to self-organize at the next level. Witness the efforts of the United Nations and the work of such organizations as the Nuclear Age Peace Foundation.

Of course, since 1945, the development of technological means of destruction or cocreation has accelerated. Through biotechnology, nanotechnology, quantum computing, space development, and other advancing technologies, we are literally able to place human intent into matter itself, terraforming planets, moving toward silicon based "life," and redesigning our own bodies. The nuclear crisis is the tip of the vast array of technological capacities for destruction or evolution. The result of technological advances, if we can learn ethical, conscious evolution, may well be, as astrophysicist Eric Chaisson says in *The Life Era*, "The establishment of a 'universal life' with all its attendant features, not the least of which potentially include species immortality and cosmic consciousness."[21]

Yet, when we allow ourselves to contemplate these possibilities, they are not totally unfamiliar. They connect us with the deepest aspirations of humanity for a higher quality of life, for transcendence of the limits of separate self-centered consciousness, planet-boundedness, and even animal life, birth and death. They reinforce the age-old dream as stated by many and simply spoken by St. Paul in the Bible: "Behold, I show you a mystery: we shall not all sleep, but we shall all be changed; in a moment in the twinkling of an eye, at the last trump, and the trumpet shall sound. . . . (1 Cor. 15:51,52) This vision is literally *coming* true.

Once again, the *new* good news is that we are in fact evolving, we *are* being changed.

THE BIRTH OF A NEW HUMANITY

The fundamental key to hope for humanity's future is that *Homo sapiens sapiens*, in our current state of consciousness, "is a transitional species," as Sri Aurobindo put it in *The Life Divine*. Perhaps we are not the final model of *Homo*. Many observers now sense that we are, right now, in transition toward a new human and a new humanity.

When we look back into the brief history (in evolutionary terms) of *Homo*, we see that we started about seven million years ago when *Australopithecus africanus* separated out from the animal world. Now visualize the sequence: *Homo erectus, Homo habilis, Homo Neanderthal, Homo sapiens, Homo sapiens sapiens*. Humans gain self-consciousness, self-reflective consciousness—a radical breakthrough in the early human world. All other *Homo's* that preceded our model are extinct. Now, 50,000 to 100,000 years later, see this current model of self-conscious humans (us!) suddenly gaining the power of gods, able to destroy or create. See us holding the atomic bombs in our hands.

Now, out of the mists of the past, reconnect with the great mystics, founders of the world's religions, those geniuses who broke through to cosmic consciousness.

See so many of us working upon ourselves to emerge beyond our self-centered egoic personalities. We are gaining *evolutionary consciousness*, a synthesis of the spiritual and the scientific, expanding our awareness to include the inner and the outer, the past, the present and the future. See us emerging as a new type of human—*Homo universalis, Homo noeticus, Homo progressivus*. All names are inadequate for the unknown type we are becoming.

In a remarkable book entitled *The Mysterious Birth Of A New Species*, Yatri writes:

> In accord with nature's upward drive towards higher and higher levels, it is possible that nature has planted perfectly developed seeds, potential functions, which lie dormant until triggered by some other biological or physiological event. As will be seen, thousands, or even millions of years could elapse while a species carries around the treasure of its future. Sometimes through an accident or a freak set of biological or cultural circumstances the seed is activated in a single individual. But nature seems to need numbers for the "seed" to take properly. It not only needs the right conditions but a minimum number of similar individuals to trigger a full evolutionary transition to a new level or a new species.[22]

One of the best words to describe this emerging human is *cocreator*. This means we are becoming ever more aware of the processes that are creating us, and are choosing to align our personal will with that deeper tendency in evolution toward higher consciousness and greater freedom. In religious language it would be called uniting our will with the will of God. In evolutionary language it is called coevolving with nature. The meaning is similar.

Many of us have some experience of this cocreative human within ourselves. We feel connected through the heart to the whole of life and are awakening to multidimensional reality. Our inner and the outer worlds are merging through intuition, higher guidance, and expanded awareness. We are aroused by profound motivation to express our creativity for the good of the self and the whole. We long to grow in love. This kind of human has been gestating in the heart of our species for thousands of years.

Today, we see that this emerging human is being called forth *en masse* for the first time in our history for the very survival of the human species. As our planetary body complexifies and interconnects, we are all being "plugged in" to the "noosphere, the mind sphere, or the thinking layer of Earth," as Teilhard de Chardin named it. Within this sphere, the global brain is awakening; the global heart is warming; the cocreative human is emerging in every discipline and faith, as the planetary conditions "heat up."

Here is another vital factor—a bio-cultural-evolutionary shift. We can no longer "be fruitful and multiply" up to maximum. As we approach the population limit on planet Earth, we *must have fewer children*. Wherever women have the choice, we are already shifting away from maximum procreation toward cocreation, from self reproduction toward self-evolution—the desire for self-actualization, self-expression, life purpose, and meaningful work. The vast energy that has gone into giving birth to and nurturing large families is becoming available for creative self-expression and concern for the larger human family, especially in women. The human/spiritual potential movement is becoming the social potential movement.

Given all this pressure to transform, we may indeed be nearing the time of a planetary awakening for a critical mass of evolving humans. We might be infusing the "morphogenetic field" described by Rupert Sheldrake as a non-physical field that is built by the behavior of a species, and affects the behavior of all members of the species. As more of us expand in consciousness and responsibility we are affecting the overall field of consciousness.[23] We may be nearing a time of mass resonance which will lead to a "global mind shift," as Willis Harman put it.

If this is possible, we are living through the time of greatest hope on Earth.

EVIL AS A STAGE OF EVOLUTION

But we cannot go further in seeking the basis of long-range hope without addressing the nature of evil. There is no doubt that humans at this stage of evolution are capable of appalling cruelty, violence, and greed. As our power increases, why would we not simply continue to misuse our power until we self-destruct?

Here is what we can see when we look at the current human condition with "evolutionary eyes." We see that evil and its twin, egotism, are stages in the evolution of humanity. They came in with self-consciousness. Animals are not evil, even though they are designed to kill one another to survive. Nature's experiment in us has been to evolve humans capable of individuality and a sense of separate identity, and with that, a moral concern and an ego that feels separate.

But in our age this process of individualization has hit a limit. If we continue in our self-centered behavior with all this power, disconnected from each other and from nature, we will destroy ourselves and our cherished freedom. However, if we are evolving toward a more whole-system consciousness—one which is empathetic, evolutionary, comprehensive and cosmic—and if we are tending to reintegrate into nature as conscious coevolvers, which I believe we are, then the root cause of evil will gradually disappear, naturally. *For that cause is the illusion that we are separate from each other, from nature and from spirit.* When we gain expanded consciousness, that illusion tends to dissolve. Because it is not true. We are really not separate. We are unique, but connected as vital parts of the living whole system. As cocreative humans, we tend to experience

reverence for life, spontaneously. Just as now we experience ourselves as "self" conscious (a great evolutionary advance), so we begin to experience ourselves as whole-centered. Empathy becomes
natural. We begin to transcend our egos by including them in this
more integrated, cooperative, universal human.[24]

This does not mean we will reach some Utopia, a word that means
no place. Rather, it means that as we cross this evolutionary threshold, we will find ourselves in a totally new set of challenges. I believe that we will be born to universal life, both on this earth and in
a universe of billions and billions of galaxies! We are literally *new-
born* cosmic beings. We have no idea of what lies in store for us as
we make it through this challenge. We are facing the "end of the
world" of self-conscious humanity, which has been overpopulating,
polluting and warring with itself on Earth. We are on the threshold
of the *next world*, which will open up for us, as we become a universal or cosmic humanity. This shift from the separated, self-centered
human to the next stage holds the promise, not of some eternal
"heaven," or extinction of self through Nirvana, but of radical new-
ness, and challenges and opportunities far greater than we can even
imagine now.

A New Developmental Path to the Next Stage of Human Evolution

If it is true that we are in the process of evolving toward a new
humanity, that we are being forced by crises and attracted by new
potentials to learn self and social evolution consciously, then what
will our developmental pathway be? What is the new "curriculum"
for conscious evolution? Hope for humanity requires that we learn
together how to coevolve and cocreate. Where are our schools for
conscious evolution?

In my work, over 35 years of research with the growing edge of
all fields, I have discovered that there is already such an emergent
path, but it has not yet been pieced together in such a way that it
has coherence.

The elements of this developmental path are an unfolding process which countless people, teachers, innovators, educators, and activists of all kinds are now creating.

Through the Foundation for Conscious Evolution, we have put this developmental path together as an educational process online called *Gateway to Our Conscious Evolution*. It is an early offering in the living "School for Conscious Evolution." As of this writing, hundreds of people are field-testing the program. We ask everyone the question: *What will it be like when a global community realizes its own potential for conscious evolution, self and social?* (See www.consciousevolution.net)

In the Gateway, we present key themes, or "portals," as an unfolding, organic participatory process that leads not to incremental change, but to quantum transformation.

Each portal is composed of critical information and knowledge that any one of us needs to participate in conscious evolution, self and social, connecting participants with a web of teachers, innovators and mentors who are already guiding thousands of people but who, until now, have been disconnected from one another.

In Portal One, *The Whole Story*, we learn the new views of the nature of the "living universe" and the story of cosmogenesis.

In Portal Two, *The Cocreative Person*, we place ourselves in cosmogenesis and see that we are an expression of that evolutionary story ourselves. We are evolving as is the universe. We make the choice to shift our identity from ego to essence, from the separated self to a connected essential self, a conscious participant in the creation.

In Portal Three, *Cocreative Relationship*, we ask ourselves: How do we actually learn to practice the Golden Rule, to love one another as ourselves? The key here is to stabilize our internal shift of identity and begin to relate to each other as essence to essence, deep self to deep self, cultivating resonance, love and forgiveness.[25]

In Portal Four, *Cocreative Vocation*, we discover that just as each of us has a genetic code, so we also have a "genius code," a soul's code, as James Hillman writes.[26] This set of unique talents presses outward from within to be more fully expressed. As we identify with our own essential selves and one another, our deeper life purpose emerges spontaneously. Participants place their "vocational profiles" in the Gateway Campus Network. The Foundation is now developing a system of helping people to connect, to find partners and teammates to fulfill their projects, fostering a social uprising of wellness and creativity.

In Portal Five, *Synergistic Community,* we realize that we cannot be fully ourselves in a dissonant commercial world. There is a growing desire for small human-scale communities where we can actually design the social/economic/political systems we choose. If we can't fix the old system, we can "transcend and create" the new. We begin the practice of a more direct and synergistic democracy that seeks the fulfillment of each person in the context of the whole, connecting with others doing the same. Bela H. Banathy calls such communities "agoras," after the 5th century Greek polis, where direct democracy was practiced.[27]

In Portal Six, *Cocreative Society,* we move from inner and small group work into society as a whole system undergoing a transition. The cocreative society would be one in which each person is free to give their gift for the good of the self and the whole. We have placed a Peace Room on line to foster connection and cooperation among the positive initiatives world wide. It is a social innovation designed to scan for, map, connect, and communicate social innovations now working. "The Peace Room" increases interactions among innovating people to facilitate the system reordering itself to a more complex and harmonious order. We are now in the process of developing an evolutionary wisdom network composed of colleagues from every field and function whose life and work is already transforming the world. They will be asked to identify innovations that are working, policies and trends that are life giving, serving guidelines for social transformation. People everywhere in the world will be invited to place their projects, needs, and resources in the Peace Room, cultivating global social synergy.

As Abraham H. Maslow first studied well people and mapped the self-actualizing person, so we begin to identify peaks of social wellness, "connecting the dots" to see the outlines of the new global wisdom culture, as it is called by the Institute of Noetic Sciences.

In Portal Seven, *Visions of a Universal Humanity,* Gateway offers a new container, a strange attractor in which each of us can place our visions until we cocreate together shared visions of our future which attract us forward to manifest them in real time. Where there is no vision, people perish. Where there is vision, people flourish.

My quest for a positive vision of our future began in 1945 when the United States dropped the atomic bombs on Japan. Stunned by the horror of that event, questions arose in my mind which have guided my life from then on. *What is the meaning of our new powers that are good? What are positive images of the future that attract us? What is the purpose of science and technology for the future of humanity?*

I discovered that no one knew the answers to these questions, the technological powers of destruction and creation were still so new. I determined to find answers myself, and have placed the results of this lifetime of research on the Gateway educational program. Now, this final portal is a place for all of us to collect our visions, our understanding of genuine new capacities, our aspirations and heart's desires.

In this portal, we invite ourselves to "land" on the other side of the chasm we are crossing in our quantum jump. We catch a glimpse of what it will be like when everything we know we can do works in harmony with that pattern in evolution toward higher consciousness and greater freedom.

With such visions, I believe that humanity will be excited once again about its own potential, as we were during the Renaissance, and the founding of democracy in the United States, and at the advent of the Enlightenment, the Scientific Age. We will find that our spiritual visions of radical transformation, expressed metaphorically as the New Jerusalem, Paradise, Nirvana, a new heaven, and a new earth, will reappear, not as spiritual intimations of life after death, but as evolutionary potentials of life after this phase of evolution. Martin Luther King, Jr.'s great inspiration, expressed in his words "I have a dream," will take hold again. *We have a dream, and it can come true through us.* We will fall in love with what we can become.

We will discover that the alternative to war is the conscious evolution of humanity, and that every one of us is needed to fulfill that cosmic enterprise.

NEW CHALLENGES, NEW POWERS

Humans have always responded to new challenges. So now, pioneers and pilgrims of the 21st century are rising and beckoning us forward to the horizon of our transformation. In this light, it is my conviction that the meaning of our crises is to activate our new potentials. The purpose of our new powers is to become a universal humanity, coevolutionary with nature and cocreative with Spirit. Our image of the future is a self-creating prophecy. As we see ourselves, so we act; as we act, so we become.

---

1 Laszlo, Ervin. 2001. *Macroshift: Navigating the Transformation to a sustainable World.* Berrett-Koehler: San Francisco, CA. p. 9,11.

2 Hubbard, Barbara Marx. 1998. *Conscious Evolution: Awakening the Power of our Social Potential.* New World Library: Novato, CA.

3 Elgin, Duane. 2000. *Promise Ahead: A vision of Hope and Action for Humanity's Future.* William Morrow: New York, p. 43-59.

4 Khan, Pir Vilayat Inayat. 1999. *Awakening: A Sufi Experience.* Jeremy P. Tarcher, Penguin Putnam Inc: New York. p. 18.

5 De Chardin, Teilhard. 1955. *The Phenomenon of Man.* Harper & Row. New York.

6 Sri Aurobindo. 1914-1920. *The Life Divine.* Lotus Press, Box 325, Twin Lakes, WE 53181, USA.

7 Khan, Pir Vilayat. Ibid.

8 Banathy, Bela H. 2000. *Guided Evolution of Society: A Systems View.* Academic/Plenum Publishers: New York.

9 Russell, Peter. 1995. *The Global Brain Awakens: Our Next Evolutionary Leap.* Global Brain: Palo Alto, CA.

10 Elgin, Duane. 1993. *Awakening Earth: Exploring the Evolution of Human Culture.* William Morrow: New York.

11 Swimme, Brian and Thomas Berry. 1994. *Universe Story: From the Primordial Flaring Forth to the Ecozoic Era.* Harper: San Francisco, CA.

12 Bache, Christopher M. 2000. *Dark Night, Early Dawn: Steps to a Deep Ecology of Mind.* State University of New York Press.

13 Sahtouris, Elisabet, Harman, Willis W. 1998. *Biology Revisited.* North Atlantic Books: Berkeley, CA.

14 Laszlo, Ervin. 1991. *The Age of Bifurcation: Understanding the Changing World.* Gordon and Breach: Philadelphia, PA.

15 Laszlo, Ervin. 1994. *The Choice: Evolution or Extinction¿* Tarcher/Putnam: New York.

16 Laszlo, Ervin. 1996. *Evolution: The General Theory.* Hampton Press: New Jersey.

17 Houston, Jean. 2000. *Jump Time: Shaping Your Future in a World of Radical Change.* Jeremy P. Tarcher, Penguin, Putnam Inc.: New York.

18 Eisler, Riane. 2002. *The Power of Partnership: Seven Relationships that Will Change Your Life.* New World Library: Novato, CA.

19 Bruteau, Beatrice. 1997. *God's Ecstasy: The Creation of a Self-Creating World.* The Crossroad Publishing Company: New York.

20 Hock, Dee. 1999. *Birth of the Chaordic Age.* Berrett-Koehler: San Francisco, CA.

21 Chaisson, Eric. 1987. *The Life Era: Cosmic Selection and Conscious Evolution.* W.W. Norton and Co.: New York. p. 224.

22 Yatri: *Unknown Man:* 1988. *The Mysterious Birth of a New Species.* A Fireside Book, Simon &Schuster Inc.: New York.

23 Sheldrake, Rupert. 1981. *A New Science of Life: The Hypothesis of Formative Causation.* J.P Tarcher, Inc.: Los Angeles. p. 76-77.

24 Hubbard, Barbara Marx. 2001. *Emergence:The Shift from Ego to Essence – Ten Steps to the Universal Human*. Hampton Roads: Charlottesville, VA.

25 Anderson, Carolyn, with Roske, Katherine. 2001. *The Co-Creator's Handbook: An Experiential guide for Discovering Your Life's Purpose and Building a Co-creative Society*. Global Family: Nevada City, CA.

26 Hillman, James. 1996. *The Soul's Code: In Search of Character and Calling.* Random House: New York.

27 Banathy, Bela H. 2000. *Guided Evolution of Society: A Systems View.* Academic/ Plenum Publishers: New York. p. 312, 356. Web site: www.21stcenturyagora.org

Unraveling the Knots

By Adam Curle

A long life has given me the opportunity to become close to a great number of people in an equally great variety of circumstances of war, turbulence, and peace, and in a vast divergency of social, cultural, and individual conditions. These varieties make for the rich pattern of human existence.

I have also found that certain recurring responses to conditions make life easier or pleasanter than it might have been. On the other hand, there are equally common responses that tend to make it less easy and pleasant. These are not abnormalities, still less mental or physical illnesses, but ways of looking at our lives which bring, or preserve, tension or dissatisfaction *unnecessarily* into our lives. They have to do with our ideas on happiness, permanence, separateness, guilt, inferiority, awareness, identity. These are so widespread (and more prevalent in some cultures and conditions than others) that their cumulative effect can make any situation explosive, even when the original grounds for hostility were trivial. I refer to these factors as *Knots*. Yet these can often be easily disentangled; in less fraught situations they may indeed pass unnoticed amongst the complex interplay of mood and behaviour. If so, however, they may still cast a slight shadow over our lives.

My own experience suggests that coping with inhibiting or even crippling Knots in our thinking, our logical understanding of our human condition, is easier and more effective, in a way more *natural*, than dealing with our problems through psychotherapy—and in any case much therapy does not touch these issues. It is largely a matter of sorting our own ideas and judging them against an obvious reality.

SOME MAJOR KNOTS

Awareness

To be awake is not necessarily to be aware. I can wake up in the morning, dress, wash, collect the papers, eat breakfast and then set off for a meeting, all without thinking, quite automatically. This machine-like capacity is, of course, very useful. My mind is absent, absorbed in some irrelevant dream and thus insulated from my environment. I am unaware that my wife is not very well. I am completely unaware of my body, of my own essence. I am oblivious of the miracle of being alive, of possessing the wonderful potential for creation and compassion with which we are all endowed.

I am like the pilot of a plane who has switched over to automatic and is having a nap. All goes well until an incident occurs for which the plane has not been programmed. In ordinary life we rely greatly on the "machine" function. I can even give a quite reasonable lecture on automatic, my mind released to think about supper or what to watch on television. All goes well until something "wakes" me, bringing my mind back. Then I realize that I do not know what point I had reached in my presentation. In particular, we need to be aware when concerned with personal or moral issues.

The great question is, how to remain awake. One answer is to ponder on the following Knots *which make us aware of our own being.*

Happiness

One of the knots concerns happiness. Seen negatively this means the absence of dismal feelings of boredom or depression; viewed positively it is a sense of pervading joy, unrelated to any particular circumstance except being alive. But there is a widely held belief that happiness depends upon circumstances wholly outside ourselves, that is to say, not in our mind. If we are not happy, we believe, it must be because of some failure in, for example, our relationships, our work, our attainments. It may even appear to be connected with our mind. For example, we may be held back because of some educational lack, but receive a promotion after further study. However, we will soon discover that, after brief euphoria, we feel much as we did before. We are driven to further, equally frustrating, efforts until we realise that happiness is the expression of inner harmony rather than satisfied ambition.

I discovered this at the age of five. I yearned for a particular toy gun which my mother, being a pacifist, refused to give me. At last, however, she yielded. At first I was overjoyed, telling myself that I would be happy forever and never want anything else. A couple of days after, however, I found myself weeping over some minor disaster. I remember well that I reasoned that the source of happiness was not external, but reflected an inner state of calm.

Identity

Another Knot concerns the identity, self, or ego. Identity is really important for us. *It is crucial for us to know who we are.* Essentially we need, when looking in the mental mirror, to be able to say that we are seeing a valid person, who may not be a saint or a genius, but who has this character and those qualities that distinguish her/him from any other human being. We tend, of course, by a process half conscious and half unconscious, to incorporate in the self-image what we consider our most attractive or laudable attributes and achievements (though we seldom realize how many friends would disagree).

When we say, "I think, I believe, I am," we make the assumption that there is a fixed entity, I, that thinks, believes, and behaves in a particular way and form that expresses solid and unique identity. It should, however, be more rightly called a *false identity.*

And even that is an incomplete answer. Honest introspection will show that we are a patchwork of often contradictory beliefs, ideas, likes, dislikes, and prejudices—of sub-personalities. But surely, we argue, there must somewhere be a super-personality, which is the "real I." We like to think so, but I have never been able to discover it.

All I know is that there are a great number of varied ideas and tendencies derived from my own experiences over many years and most varied circumstances. These tendencies, these sub-I's, some pleasant, some very unpleasant, surface in different circumstances. A different "I" emerges when my body is at a cheerful party, or with people I want to impress, or if I am with people I love. In all these circumstances a different "I" crawls from the mental woodwork, triggering depression or self-satisfied elation, or fear, or bragging, or many of the myriad other selves and their affiliates.

In fact, every time we say that we believe, or think such and such, we tell a lie—no, perhaps not a lie but a half truth, for we are saying what only one of the sub-I's thinks or believes at a particular moment. Tomorrow, in different company, and in a fractionally changed world, or stimulated by a slightly different setting, another sub-I may surface with another opinion.

Am I then propounding a sort of nihilism? Not at all. I am only saying that the "I" we attribute to ourselves is a fiction. But our friends know a different, a more genuine, I. If we could see and accept ourselves as others see us, we would have a better idea of what (who) we are. But our illusions about our identity and about the nature of happiness shield us from reality. Moreover they expose us to the disappointments and frustrations which inevitably beset us if we try to fabricate identity from fictitious qualities or transient interests. Moreover, each frustration increases our desperation and despair, thus driving us to adopt further illusions.

Our psychic path is paved with vicious circles.

Permanence

One of these circles relates to the illusion of permanence. We tend to *feel*—not to know, because of course the intellect would reject the idea—that a period of life in which we are contented will remain unchanged and that we will live in it forever. Many of us marry, *feeling* that our bliss will be unending, but finish up in the divorce courts. But of course nothing in the universe is unending, including naturally our own lives. Moreover, paradoxically, we

84

would not wish it so; who would want an unhappy relationship or a tedious occupation to last forever?

Nevertheless, when I return home after an absence, I have the strong *inner feeling* that I am coming back to a haven of peace and stability. But I am also aware that I may find the house has been burgled or burned down, that my wife is in hospital, or that some other disaster has struck. This subjective conflict vitiates the calmness of my mind; fundamentally I am afraid of death and am searching for an immortality I know to be an illusion. I strive mentally to believe in permanence, but am faced constantly with the fact of failure. To escape from my failures I indulge in absurd emotional or intellectual caprices. I rely on my ego to search out any fantasy of glory or power in which my fears are temporarily obliterated, my confusion forgotten.

But of course I can only find peace, stability and real purpose in the acceptance of impermanence and death; only then can I know the deep joys of just living without the hobbling crutches of expectation.

Separateness

The conventional idea of ego, the self, I, is of a separate, self-existing, autonomous individual. This is something else we learn from our earliest years to *feel*. To a considerable extent contemporary Western society is built on the concepts of the separate, autonomous individual. Other cultures are less firmly based on individualism, but probably all humans, and perhaps other sorts of beings, have strong feelings about what happens to them as separate entities.

However, if we return to the elements that make up identity, it is clear, culture apart, that we cannot split off Bill Smith from the genetic and social influence of his parents and other ancestors and other family members. Or from what he has acquired from his teachers, reading, friends, work, and the total ambience in which he has lived at various stages in his life. He is as he is because they are as they are, and indeed the other way around. In one sense we are all interconnected; in another we are intrinsically individual: each of us is a miracle of unity in diversity and diversity in unity.

Guilt and Inferiority

Our constantly fluctuating false identities veer (in varying degrees for us all) between the grandiose and the abysmal. At one level we feel we are angels, at another we feel we are worms. We often feel guilty for our low awareness; we dimly feel that we are somehow failing, like the man in the Gospel parable, to invest our innate talents, and so are worthless.

In fact, we all, even the physically impaired, have powers and abilities almost beyond our imagination. But these are dimmed and suppressed in the process of socialization. What could we do if the full possibilities of our nature were not limited by our failure to recognize them; what could we achieve if our capacities were not limited by misunderstanding them, or by whittling away our energies in needless and negative emotion such as worry, fear, self-pity, envy, and yearning?

Violence

There is a widespread belief in the great majority of cultures that, when all other methods of resolving a quarrel have failed, violence is a legitimate last resort. If this general principle is queried, a frequent riposte is that it is a natural feral instinct. But human violence, so cruel, irrational, and implacable, differs greatly from animal violence, which is pragmatically directed towards a limited practical goal such as securing a mate or protecting young. We seldom have any practical *need* for violence. Nevertheless, it is, or has become, a human habit—a bad one.

There are two aspects of this issue. The first is that the resolution of any conflict by violent means causes suffering and damage. This, especially in the case of war, can monstrously exceed, as hindsight often shows, the hurt caused by the original quarrel. The second is that a quarrel brought to an end by violence is hardly ever actually ended. If peace is imposed by victory of one protagonist over another, or through the intervention of a powerful third party, little may be achieved beyond an end of the fighting; the people may still hate each other, the old grudges still remain. But harmony and justice, by which truth is to be recognized, may still be as distant as ever.

But there are other ways that are at least as intrinsic to our nature as violence. This may be most readily discovered by cutting through the Knots and recognizing that much of what we tend to believe about our nature is untrue or at least ambiguous. This liberation from illusion empowers the wisdom and compassion that loosen the stranglehold of conflict and violence on our minds. This, of course, has been demonstrated by a few great human beings such as Mahatma Gandhi, and many less well-known, some of whom I have been privileged to meet.

BRINGING ABOUT CHANGE

It may appear strange that in considering something so momentous as the future of humanity we should mainly be talking about the feelings, not necessarily profound or important, of individuals. Surely it is much more important to discuss the structure of international relations, the global economy, interracial tensions, etc. Well, yes, I agree. But these are matters we can personally or directly do little about, and there are many able and competent people who can. But we as individuals can make a difference to ourselves and in so doing, to those around us. And it is important to remember that it is the masses of the people who bring about the big changes—for good or for bad.

Our Power for Peace

By Daisaku Ikeda

Never doubt that a small group of thoughtful, committed people can change the world; indeed, it is the only thing that ever has.

I am very fond of these words of the great American anthropologist Margaret Mead, for they express a profound and enduring truth.

To young people in particular I wish to say: The world is yours to change. Your dreams, your hopes and aspirations—these will create the future. They are the future. The future already exists—in the hearts and minds of the young.

The New Superpower

However hard it may be to believe, each of us is infinitely powerful. We have the power, individually and collectively, to change the world. As Nobel Peace Laureate Jody Williams and others have said, together the so-called "ordinary citizens" of the world are a superpower. We the people are the new superpower.

What are the keys to unleashing that power, bringing it to bear on the task of creating a world of peace? There are four aspects that I think are especially important: Power of Hope; Power of Imagination; Power of Connection; and Power of Dialogue.

The Power of Hope

Sometimes hopes and dreams are spoken of as something fragile and easily broken. In fact, they are anything but that. The power of hope and dreams is the power from which the world is born new each day. The more noble, the more compassionate and humane the goal toward which our hope is directed, the greater the power we bring forth from within. Nothing is more profoundly empowering than the determination to work for peace—the hope that has been cherished in the hearts of countless generations of humanity.

There are those who tell us that humanity is condemned to war and violence, that it is ingrained in our nature to hate and kill each other. Such people will tell you that they are simply being "realistic." I sincerely hope that you will never submit to such "realism"— not about your own lives, not about the world. If you examine such claims carefully, you will usually find that those who make them have simply decided—in an arbitrary and often self-serving way—what is realistic and what is not. They cut off and deny the limitless possibilities of reality to make it fit with their own pessimism and narrow-mindedness.

President Kennedy clearly rejected pessimism about peace when he said, "We need not accept that view. Our problems are manmade. Therefore, they can be solved by man.... No problem of human destiny is beyond human beings."

Every war has started in the human heart. And so has every great act that has changed the world for the better.

The leadership to free the world from the threat of nuclear weapons, to build a world without war, is to be found in "ordinary" people like us. So it is vital that we never forget that we can build such a world, that we are the protagonists of the drama of human history.

In Japanese, the word for "hope" is written with two Chinese characters. One means to desire something deeply and intensely. The other means to gaze far into the distance, into the future.

Mahatma Gandhi was, in his own words, an "irrepressible optimist." But his hope was not based on an objective analysis of the conditions that faced him. Rather, it was based on his absolute faith in the "infinite possibilities of the individual." In the same way, the great dream of equality and human dignity that possessed Martin Luther King, Jr., was a dream upheld by the force of diamond-like faith and will.

All those who have achieved great things have done so because of their ability to create hope, to pull it forth from within themselves, regardless of the circumstances or challenges they face. We must learn to make the hope we cannot find. Where there is hope, there is the possibility of peace.

THE POWER OF IMAGINATION

I also want to stress the power of imagination, for this is the "bridge" across which our ideals travel to become new realities.

Imagination is the wellspring from which hope flows. It is the power of imagination, the power to imagine different realities, that frees us from the mistaken notion that what exists now is all that will ever exist, and that we are trapped inside our problems.

Everything changes. Nothing is "written in stone," fixed and unchanging for all time—not even the stone itself. The Greek philosopher Heraclitus expressed this saying, we can never step in the same river twice. The water flows without cease and what we set foot in a moment ago is already gone, replaced by a new flow.

Since everything changes, the real question is whether it will change for the better or for the worse. And that, finally, is up to us. If our hearts are filled with hatred and despair, that is the world we will create. If our hearts are filled with hope and compassion, we can without fail create a better, more peaceful world.

The power of imagination is also the power of empathy. It is the ability to imagine, the willingness to feel the pain of others. It is the spirit that says, "So long as you are suffering, whoever you are and whatever your suffering may be, I suffer also." The scale of our empathy—reaching out to those in distant places, to people whose lifestyles and language may be different from our own—is the scale of our humanity. A life of true fulfillment is one marked by the non-stop effort to expand and deepen one's humanity. Our capacity to feel the pain of others is perhaps the surest gauge of where we stand in that ongoing effort.

When the realists tell us to accept a world of suffering, a world of war and injustice, what they are really doing is displaying the stagnation and failure of their own imagination.

I firmly believe that peace education—education that stirs empathetic imagination by conveying the realities of war—is our shared responsibility. All sectors of society, the schools, the media and religious institutions, can play a part. In particular, I hope that young people will learn never to be deceived by sanitized or glorified portrayals of violence and war.

THE POWER OF CONNECTION

The limitless power of the individual is unleashed when we work together. This is the power of connection, the power of human solidarity. Our dreams grow and flourish when we speak them out loud, when we share them with others. To do this requires courage. We must overcome the fear that we will be misunderstood, looked down on or laughed at for putting into words the content of our hearts.

The solidarity of the world's so-called ordinary citizens holds the key to peace. The Buddhist people's movement of the Soka Gakkai, from which the SGI has grown, was founded in Japan in 1930 by an educator named Tsunesaburo Makiguchi. In his writings, he noted that evil-minded people, aware of their inner deficiencies, are quick to band together. People of good will, on the other hand, are spiritually more self-sufficient and therefore do not feel so strong a need for allies. As a result, they are often overwhelmed and defeated by people of evil intent. Only when people of good will unite can we change the world.

Wars are almost always described as a struggle of one country against another, of one people or group against another. In fact, however, they are started by leaders who are trying to fill the gaping void they feel inside—their own sense of powerlessness—by controlling and commanding others. The time has come for the world's ordinary citizens to unite in resisting those who promote violence, terrorism, and war. The time has come for humanity to unite in rejecting violence in all its forms. This is the vision that motivated the youth members of SGI-USA to start their "Victory Over Violence" campaign, a grassroots effort to empower people to resist and overcome violence in their lives and in the world.

THE POWER OF DIALOGUE

In the end, peace will not be realized by politicians signing treaties. True and lasting peace will only be realized by forging life-to-life bonds of trust and friendship among the world's people. Human solidarity is built by opening our hearts to each other. This is the power of dialogue.

Dialogue is more, however, than two people facing each other speaking. The kind of dialogue that can truly contribute to peace must begin with an open and earnest "inner dialogue." By this I mean the ability to examine, carefully and honestly, our own attitudes.

We can start by asking ourselves some simple questions: Have I made the effort to find out the facts? Have I confirmed things for myself? Have I been swayed by second-hand information, by stereotypes or malicious rumors?

For Socrates, a clear awareness of one's own ignorance was the starting point for wisdom. By questioning ourselves and our assumptions we can open the way to more meaningful communication. This is something that applies at all levels—from communications between family and friends, to those between countries and cultures. This is because people who are at least aware that they may harbor prejudicial attitudes can communicate across differences more successfully than those who are convinced that they are free from all prejudice.

Ultimately, the challenge we each face is to grow into the kind of person who is capable of truly respecting others.

In the teachings of Buddhism there is a passage that describes what our attitude toward people should be. It says that we should "rise and greet them from afar," showing them the utmost respect. In fact, it states that we should offer them the same respect we would a Buddha. Here I should clarify that a "Buddha" is not a superhuman being. Rather, this word refers to a person who has fully awakened the limitless capacity for wisdom and compassion that exists in all people. It is another way of expressing the supreme dignity that all people possess simply by virtue of being human.

How could there be war if we saw each meeting with another as a rare and remarkable encounter with the most precious treasure of the cosmos? I can think of no more direct and simple path to peace.

HUMAN REVOLUTION

The second president of the Soka Gakkai, Josei Toda, was the person I look to as my mentor in life. Together with founding president Makiguchi, he was imprisoned for opposing the policies of Japan's militarist government during World War II. President Makiguchi died in prison in November 1944. Mr. Toda was released a little more than a month before Japan surrendered in August 1945. Mr. Toda called the process of fundamentally transforming our lives "human revolution." Caring deeply for others, he worked tirelessly to empower ordinary citizens, to awaken them to the treasures of wisdom and strength they carry within.

It was his belief, one that I have taken up as the core theme of my own work for peace, that a great revolution in the life of a single individual can change an entire society. It can even make possible a positive transformation in the destiny of humankind. This is the kind of power for peace we each possess.

The Social Responsibility of Scientists

By Sir Joseph Rotblat

I t should be clear that science has acquired an extraordinary status. It has become a major factor in shaping the lives of individuals and the destiny of mankind. Further advances in science and technology can provide the means to improve enormously the lot of people—better health, more wealth, greater opportunities for cultural enrichment. It can also provide the means for more efficient and cheaper extermination, the tools to bring about the extinction of the human species.

Such tools, nuclear weapons, are already in existence, but they may not be the only instruments of wholesale destruction that man can devise. Other areas of scientific research, for example, genetic engineering, which seems to be growing at an alarming rate, could lead to such an instrument. We have to assume and make it a working principle that, in the absence of effective, preventive action, other technical means of extinguishing the human species will be invented. Some may be more easily available than nuclear weapons.

We have to come to terms with the fact that the human species is now an endangered species. The preservation of the human species must be our top priority. We must not allow the miraculous product of billions of years of evolution to come to an end because we cannot forget our quarrels. We are beholden to our ancestors, to all the previous generations who bequeathed to us the immense cultural heritage that we enjoy. It is our duty to pass it on to future generations. We owe an allegiance to humanity.

THE DUTY OF SCIENTISTS

Nurturing such an allegiance is the duty of each of us, of every citizen, but the duty falls especially heavily on the scientists because the main threat to humanity is likely to arise from the work of scientists. I believe that scientists are more likely to bring about such catastrophe. I'll give you examples of the work that scientists are doing now to avert such a catastrophe.

I am taking this from a statement by Sir Michael Atiya, a scientist of great distinction who succeeded me as president of the Pugwash Conferences on Science and World Affairs. He puts forward these points:

- Scientists will understand the technical problems better than the average politician or citizen, and knowledge brings responsibility.

- Remember this, that you have knowledge and you are responsible for how this knowledge is properly used. Scientists can provide technical advice and assistance for solving the incidental problems that may emerge.

- Scientists can warn of further dangers that may arise from current discoveries. Scientists can form an international fraternity that transcends beyond natural boundaries, so they are well placed to take a global view in the interest of mankind.

The conferment of these responsibilities on scientists may be considered as enforced limitations on scientific research. An ethical course of conduct in scientific research has been set up by international bodies of scientists. Such bodies will require universal adherence, because there is little use of guidelines that are adhered to in some countries and ignored in others.

Again, speaking in a scientific environment, I acknowledge that a control on science is almost a contradiction in terms. Scientific research is the pursuit of the unknown. By its very nature, science has to be completely free. However, the potential cataclysmic consequences of scientific research make it imperative to impose some limitations, at least until we've learned to conduct our affairs peacefully and to settle our disputes without resorting to military confrontation.

A HIPPOCRATIC OATH FOR SCIENTISTS

Certain areas of research are already subject to controls. For example, medical research projects which involve experiments on patients have to be approved by hospital ethical committees, which may reject them if they do not meet certain ethical criteria. It seems to me that the time has come, as you would have heard from my Nobel speech, for scientists to adopt some form of Hippocratic Oath. The Hippocratic Oath now applies to medical people; I'm talking about making such an oath binding on *all* scientists.

I acknowledge that any limitation on the scientist's freedom will be strongly resisted. Every scientist has to realize that he or she is first of all a citizen; and that the interests of the world community must be paramount. In any case, if scientists do not put their house in order themselves it will be enforced on them by the state by popular demand.

There has been an outcry about cloning. All of you are familiar with Dolly the Sheep and how her cloning can be extrapolated to the possibility of human cloning. This outcry is an indication of what possible reactions are likely.

In the United States, the student Pugwash group has organized a pledge for young scientists to take when they begin their scientific career. It states:

> I promise to work for a better world where science and technology are used in socially responsible ways. I will not use my education to any purpose to harm human beings or the environment. Throughout my career I will consider the ethical implications of my work before I take action. While the demands placed on me may be

great, I sign this declaration because I recognize that individual responsibility is the first step on the path to peace.

These young people are enthusiastic. I hope that this pledge will
become part of the degree ceremony for anyone who qualifies.

For the older scientists, we also have similar requests. The most
senior scientist of the Manhattan Project, Hans Bethe, a Nobel Laureate who had worked on the Manhattan Project and later became
an advisor and consultant to Los Alamos, came out with an appeal
to scientists to desist from work on weapons of mass destruction.
Coming from him, it should have a big effect on the scientific community.

Even so, I expect that there will be much resistance. Yet, I'm afraid
that if we don't do it, there is danger of an anti-science attitude
among the public. Science has acquired a bad public image. Scientists themselves are partly to blame, by embarking on these new
areas which the public finds repulsive.

THE PUGWASH MOVEMENT

I have been involved in raising the conscience of scientists now
for forty years in the Pugwash Movement, which is an amorphous
group without organization. There is no membership in Pugwash.
People are invited individually for each particular topic. The main
purpose of Pugwash is explained in this sentence which was adopted
by our Council:

"The Pugwash Movement is an expression of the awareness of
the social and moral duty of scientists to help to prevent and overcome the actual and potential harmful effects of scientific and technological innovations; and to promote the use of science and
technology for the purpose of peace."

Pugwash is not open to all scientists for a practical reason.
Pugwash is not a mass movement, but a forum for debate. It is an
opportunity for a small number to come together, present arguments,
come up with original ideas, and try to convince each other. This
can only be done in private sessions. Most of our activities are work-

shops in which about 25 to 30 people participate at a time. They are closed to the press and the media not because we are a secret society, but simply because we are trying to create an atmosphere conducive to a free exchange of ideas. New scientific ideas may sound half-crazy; we need the freedom to work them through and find their good qualities. If the press were present, they would jump on the early ideas and write about them before they were worked out.

Once a year we have a larger meeting, maybe 150 people or something of this sort. Even then we divide ourselves into about six groups which sit around a table and then we come together for an exchange of views. Having said that there is no international membership for Pugwash, I should add that there are national groups, and there are people who attend only national conferences. In the United States the national Pugwash group is linked with the American Academy of Arts and Science in Cambridge.

We have been working as a group for more than forty years. Most of our efforts have been concentrated during this period on getting rid of weapons of mass destruction—chemical weapons, biological weapons, and primarily nuclear weapons—because they present the most immediate danger. Halting the arms race and preventing a nuclear war have been our chief involvements. Many other people contributed, but we must have played some role in it, since the Nobel committee recognized this as worthy of an award, a Nobel Peace Prize.

Eventually we have to tackle the main dangers to humanity. This can only come about if we eliminate all war, not just nuclear war but all war.

I set myself two objectives in my life. One is a short-term objective and the other is a long-term objective. The short-term objective is the elimination of nuclear weapons; the long-term objective is the elimination of all war. I hope to live to see the first objective. I'm not sure about the second.

At the very first meeting of the Pugwash Movement, which was held in Nova Scotia at Pugwash forty-five years ago, this is what we expressed:

"The principal objective of all nations must be the abolition of war and the threat of war hanging over mankind. War must be finally eliminated, not merely regulated by limiting the weapons which may be used."

SCIENTISTS MUST TAKE ACTION

In conclusion, let me mention that although I am now over 90 years old, I don't generally dwell on my past. I always look forward. Occasionally, however, I have to look back to not only the forty-five years of my work in Pugwash, but another forty years back when I was a young child and began to comprehend the world around me. At that time I developed a tremendous enthusiasm for science—science not only as a supreme expression of the human intellect but as the means to alleviate the miseries of life (hunger and disease, squalor and degradation, prejudice and cruelty, and the scourge of war). As a child I fervently believed that science could and would put an end to all this evil. Looking back now at the dream of a child, I'm glad to know that much of it has come true.

On the whole, the world is infinitely better off than it was at the beginning of the twentieth century. Much, perhaps most, of this betterment is due to the progress of science. But I also have to note with sadness that science itself has become perverted in some of its pursuits, above all in having provided the means to bring all human life to an end.

Scientists themselves can restore the proper image of science by devoting themselves to its true calling, which in the words of Francis Bacon, nearly 400 years ago, should be not for the pleasure of the mind, but for the benefit and use of life, and to subdue and overcome the miseries of humanity.

Creating a Center for Humanity's Future

By Frank K. Kelly

P eople all over the Earth are gradually awakening to the most astounding aspects of human beings—that we are not only parts of the mysterious universe, we are embodiments of the whole cosmos, each of us absolutely original and unique but limitless in our capacity. We are finite individuals and yet we will affect everything that happens in the future.

In this century the discoveries of the human mind—the release of nuclear energy and other revelations—have brought us to the brink of annihilation. In the same century, we have demonstrated enormous cruelty and enormous compassion. We have created a global communications system in which human beings reach out to one another across all boundaries of time and space. Ideas flash around the world, reshaping old institutions and bringing new ones into existence.

To serve the global community now arising through the individual efforts of people all over the planet, I believe there will be a great opportunity for the fostering and celebration of human creativity through a Center for Humanity's Future. I advocate the formation of such a Center as a statement of confidence in the tremendous productive capacities of human beings—as a place of light and listening, a place of exploration and encouragement, a launching pad for ideas from throughout the world.

That Center could have the bold spirit that marked the Center for the Study of Democratic Institutions, which blazed across the world's horizons from 1959 to 1981 with the many projects it launched from its headquarters in Santa Barbara. It helped to prevent a war between the United States and the Soviet Union. It was a pioneer in the environmental movement. It called attention to the destructive potentialities of television. It published a model for a new American Constitution, designed to protect human liberties and to indicate human responsibilities in the future. It brought together thousands of people in dialogues and conferences in Santa Barbara, Chicago, New York, Washington, Malta, and Geneva. It became an "early warning system" for humanity.

The preamble for the proposed model for a new Constitution for the United States contained a declaration that it was designed "to welcome the future in good order." In our time, we have become intensely concerned with "the future." All organizations have "vision statements" and make plans for the next years, the next decades, the next century, or even longer.

Welcoming the future in good order should be one of the primary purposes of the new Center. For many people, the future has a menacing aspect—with imagined disasters and catastrophes rushing toward us. The Center could give a continuing emphasis to the positive possibilities, while recognizing the negative ones.

THE IMPORTANCE OF CELEBRATION

In the coming age, in which human beings will face more complex problems and more challenges than ever before, it will be essential to evoke the positive powers inherent in every person. That is why the proposed Center should be dedicated to celebration—to foster the release of everyone's highest thoughts and emotional intelligence.

Celebration means more than a never-ending party, or fun and games all year round, although it does include all the aspects of joy, because human beings are at their best when they are joyful, when they take delight in everything to which they are related in a mysterious unfolding universe.

A Center for Humanity's Future could raise the banner of celebration over the whole Earth—bringing together people of all kinds in meetings and dialogues, honoring the fine work going on in many places by creative and compassionate persons, inviting everyone to open up and communicate in many languages through the Internet and other channels, lauding the value of cooperation, encouraging everyone to "welcome the future in good order."

OVERCOMING THE POWER OF VIOLENCE

In addition to honoring and promoting the positive potentialities of all human beings, the Center could explore and advocate every possible step to overcome the power of violence. With the existence of nuclear weapons and other instruments of mass destruction, the continuation of life on Earth is at stake.

The costs of violence in the twentieth century have been colossal. Millions of lives have been destroyed in the countless wars which have occurred. The Holocaust revealed the destructive depths to which human beings could descend. The massacres in Africa, Yugoslavia, Asia, and elsewhere have been horrifying in their ferocity— the extermination of neighbors by neighbors, the tortures and slaughters of women, children, and old people, have shown cruelties on a staggering scale.

One of the primary purposes of the Center could be to examine the strategies used in human efforts to reduce or eliminate violence. The admonitions of religious leaders, the development of severe punishments under strict laws, the therapeutic programs of psychologists have not been very effective.

A six-point pledge developed by the United Nations Education and Scientific Organization (UNESCO) would be offered for consideration. The points are:

1. Respect all life

2. Reject violence in all its forms, particularly violence directed at the most deprived and vulnerable people

3. Share with others, in a spirit of generosity

4. Listen to understand

5. Preserve the planet

6. Rediscover solidarity

This pledge is based on the realization that everyone must take a personal share of responsibility for the future of humanity.

Widening Roles for Women in Shaping Humanity's Future

The Center for the Study of Democratic Institutions was almost exclusively a male enterprise, dominated by highly active men with elitist ideas of leadership. Only one woman was ever appointed to the scholarly circle—the Fellows—who ran the Center.

The increasing activities of women in all fields certainly has crucial significance for the future of the human species. A Center dedicated to humanity's future must give the widest scope to women, who now compose 52 percent of the world's population. From its board of directors to its staff, such a Center must have women fully represented.

Since that Center will be continuously engaged in initiating, receiving, discussing, and promoting ideas for the benefit of humanity, women around the world will be continuously invited to take part in the life of the Center. There will be a place for everybody at the Center's table. There will be a physical table, located in the Center's headquarters in Santa Barbara—but the table will extend around the planet through the Internet and other methods of communication.

Hearing from People of All Ages: the Lifting of Every Voice

The idea of a great circle around the world, with people of all ages speaking and listening to one another, has seemed to be a fantasy—until our time, when it has become a reality. Human beings are now crossing all geographic boundaries easily and swiftly.

The Center for Humanity's Future would invite participants in all the dialogues already under way to comment on the principal topics offered by the Center for worldwide discussion. The first topics could be:

- Overcoming the power of violence, preventing war, and building a culture of peace;

- Awakening everyone to the primacy of individual persons in shaping the future;

- Recognizing the spiritual dimensions of every human being and encouraging spiritual growth;

- Reaffirming the necessity for protecting the environment and maintaining the earth as a flourishing home for all forms of life;

- Emphasizing the need for cooperation as an instrument for achieving the good of all;

- Exploring what it means to be human in the 21st Century; and

- Developing a Code of Human Responsibilities.

In the Center's outreach to people of all ages, there could be a continuous reminder of the fact that every human being has an impact on the future and will have an influence felt for many generations.

PRESENTING AN ANNUAL REPORT ON THE STATE OF HUMANITY—AND A GLOBAL CELEBRATION OF CREATIVITY

Each year, the Center could present an Annual Report on the State of Humanity, based on the ideas flowing into it and from it throughout the year. People everywhere might be asked to pledge their support for the international movement for the formation of a culture of peace and nonviolence.

The Center could also sponsor a global Celebration of Creativity, highlighting the marvelous achievements of women, men, children and people from all backgrounds. Artists of all kinds—musicians, dancers, singers, poets, mystics, doctors, healers, prophets, sculptors—could lead community celebrations which would be linked together around the world. It would recognize the creativity of everyone—and the connections of human beings with one another. It could be videotaped and used on television and the Internet to bring delight into the daily lives of people everywhere.

The Center itself could be a fountain of joy and inspiration—with its mission to foster hope and happiness and sing a great song as Beethoven did—a song of confidence in the strength and wide-ranging abilities of human beings, aware of their tremendous roles in a universe filled with limitless creativity.

CITIZENSHIP AND DEMOCRACY

The Responsibilities of World Citizenship

By Queen Noor al Hussein

More and more every day, by necessity, we are all becoming World Citizens. Daily we are witnessing the dissolution of borders—political, economic, ecological. My husband, King Hussein, among many other things, was a keen pilot, and flying with him taught me the irrelevance of national boundaries. From the air, it is clear that lines on the map are not drawn in the earth. And with modern technical advances, it is possible to communicate instantaneously, independent of any terrestrial borders at all.

In the midst of the rush caused by our rapidly shrinking world, it is worth stopping for a moment to ponder what world citizenship means. We all share the same problems and must be part of the same solutions. Globalization increases opportunities, yes, but for exploitation as well as for growth. World citizenship implies sharing cultures and benefits, but also risks and responsibilities. Recognizing we are all citizens of the world is the first step towards peace.

Being a citizen of the world means realizing that as the world shrinks, there is less and less room on it for weapons and arms, whether in the hands of governments, insurgent groups, or individuals. King Hussein said a quarter century ago: "Nothing is more useless in developing a nation's economy than a gun, and nothing blocks the road to social development more than the financial burden of war. War is the archenemy of national progress and the modern scourge of civilized man." As we see all too clearly in our region, where the spending on armaments is the highest per capita in the world, this is a colossal waste of valuable resources, monetary, material, and human.

The presence and availability of these vast arsenals, rather than acting as a deterrent, actually makes it harder to establish a lasting peace. If channeled into human priorities instead, such resources would provide much more sustainable forms of social security as a defense against violence. And it is not just officially sanctioned wars that cause such devastation. In the first half of this century wars were mammoth struggles between superpowers; and now longstanding ethnic tensions have escaped the restraints of larger state controls, escalating into conflicts smaller, more localized, but no less devastating to those caught up in them. The world is becoming both more global and more fragmented. Such conflicts have repercussions far outside their geographical boundaries. One of the most insidious effects of globalization is that it has extended the reach of terrorism with the ready availability of all sorts of destructive agents, from loose nukes to chemicals to explosives to small arms and the increased ability to move materials and people anywhere in the world. Truly, no one is safe any longer from a splinter group with a grievance and no conscience.

NUCLEAR TERRORISM

One of the greatest evils in terms of lost resources and the danger of lost lives is nuclear weapons. With the end of the Cold War some people may have felt that we could breathe easier, that the danger of nuclear annihilation had receded; but this is no time for complacency about perhaps the single greatest threat that has ever faced humankind.

As we have seen with the entry of India and Pakistan into the nuclear club, the increased possibility of instability or accident in the Russian military, and the destabilizing influence of the clandestine nuclear programs of Israel and Iraq, the dangers are only proliferating. Some 1.8 tons of explosive power for every person on earth raises to new heights the definition of overkill. There has been a great deal of concern in recent years about terrorism and chemical and biological weapons of mass destruction, but what are nuclear arms if not the archetypal weapon of mass destruction? What is a defense policy based on the threat to murder countless innocent civilians but terrorism on a massive scale!

Nuclear weapons have been declared illegal under international law by the International Court of Justice. They must be considered immoral by anyone with a conscience. The sheer folly of trying to defend a nation by destroying all life on the planet must be apparent to anyone capable of rational thought. Nuclear capability must be reduced to zero, globally, permanently. There is no other option.

Anti-Personnel Landmines

Less dramatic but perhaps much more of a day-to-day threat in the lives of millions is another type of weapon, anti-personnel mines. These pose a more insidious threat to civilians and progress because they continue killing after the conflict has stopped. When peace is declared, the guns and mortars are stilled, but no one turns off the mines. And because they are small, and destroy lives one by one, their horrific consequences can go as unnoticed as the mines themselves.

You may by now be familiar with the ghastly statistics: some 300,000 people around the globe are living with shattered limbs and lives, and the number is growing! Every month around 800 people are killed and 1,200 maimed by landmines—primarily civilians, often children attracted by their toy-like shapes and colors—a new tragedy every 20 minutes.

These indiscriminate killers constitute one of the greatest public health hazards of the early twenty-first century—a modern man-made epidemic. As Patron of the Landmine Survivors Network and international spokesperson for the International Campaign to Ban Landmines (ICBL), I have visited with survivors in the Middle East, United States, Vietnam, and Cambodia. I have seen first-hand the devastation caused by loss of life and limb. The only way to relieve the suffering of the survivors of landmines is to rid the world of landmines, and achieve universal compliance with the Ottawa Convention.

Fortunately, over the past few years we have witnessed the growth of a new coalition, activism which brought into force, in record time, the Ottawa Landmine Ban Treaty, the first international arms treaty to encompass humanitarian obligations to the weapons' victims. Working together in unprecedented networks, concerned nations, organizations, and individuals are united in a pledge to win back blighted land, to fulfill our humanitarian responsibilities to the survivors, and to make peace on the ground a reality as well as a declaration. Inspired by this progress, Jordan hosted in July 1998 the first Middle East Conference on Landmines Injury & Rehabilitation, where I was proud to announce that Jordan was signing the Ottawa Convention, which we subsequently ratified. The conference brought together from throughout the Middle East and North Africa the largest group of landmine casualties ever gathered in one place.

My country was an unfortunately appropriate place to convene, because the Middle East is littered with, by estimates, more than half of the world's deployed landmines. In Jordan, children and adults are routinely injured, and about ten percent of our population lives in areas still dangerous and economically unproductive because of landmines. Scarce agricultural lands and some of the most beautiful and sacred historic landscapes in the country, especially in the biblical Jordan River Valley, were scarred and forbidden until recently.

Events in the news have re-emphasized both the urgency of the fight against landmines, and the tremendous progress we have made. The first of these was the horrific flooding in Mozambique. Not only did it leave nearly one million people homeless, threatened by disease and starvation, but in some areas, the floodwaters uncovered buried mines and washed them from marked minefields to new areas, previously thought of as safe. In 1998 Nicaragua faced the same threat as a result of hurricanes. In these tragic cases, natural disasters joined with man-made ones, therefore posing new and heightened threats to already suffering peoples.

There have been more hopeful signs. In March 2000, His Holiness Pope John Paul II visited Jordan and made a pilgrimage to

Bethany, the baptismal site of Jesus Christ. His visit would have been inconceivable only a few short years ago, for the area was then heavily mined. There was a sad irony that landmines should hold hostage one of the world's most spiritually significant landscapes, revered by Judaism, Christianity, and Islam.

Since 1993, we have cleared the Jordan Valley of some 300,000 mines, to allow those who had tilled the land many years ago to cultivate it again, and others to unearth once more our region's precious history. And now, pilgrims who wish to walk in the paths of the prophets can do so in safety. This ancient and holy land is no longer desecrated by mines. The Prophet Mohammed said, "imatatu al-'atha 'an al-tareeq sadaqah," that "the removal of harmful objects from the path is a good deed." What was once a metaphorical, moral precept is now a literal necessity—a prophecy that has become too true for comfort.

ARMS TRADE AND GLOBAL SAFETY

In a few short years the fight to eradicate landmines has gone from a noble dream to international law, but landmines are only the tip of an iceberg in the problem of armaments of every kind, from nuclear weapons to handguns. Small arms in particular pose a growing threat to conflict prevention and recovery. The indiscriminate sale and distribution of easily carried weapons is the source of a broad spectrum of violence, from schoolyard shootings to civil wars to militia-led genocide, threatening daily the lives of more people than any other menace.

Encouraged first by progress in banning weapons of mass destruction, and then by the unprecedented success of the movement to ban landmines, the Red Cross and other concerned groups have launched similar initiatives against small arms proliferation. Controlling such arms is essential to any lasting peace anywhere in the world; but it is by no means simple. As Martin Amis put it, "weapons are like money; nobody knows the meaning of enough."

What is more, in many cases weapons are money. The arms trade, both legal and illicit, is a source of tremendous profits, from the military-industrial giants through the gun-runners down to the de-commissioned soldier who sells his weapon back on the black market. Often, ironically, a declaration of peace in one conflict will lead to an escalation of violence in neighboring countries, as weapons filter from former combatants to informal militias or criminal gangs. Small arms are cheap, easy to obtain and difficult to trace. They hold a place in the psyche of many cultures that makes them almost impossible to dislodge. From rural America to Albania to Northern Ireland to Kosovo, the unwillingness to give up guns by those who feel they are their only protection is one of the greatest threats to peace.

SUPRA-NATIONAL STRUCTURES FOR GLOBAL SAFETY

In our rapidly shrinking world, national sovereignty must acknowledge supra-national structures to ensure global safety, just as individuals must recognize the need for balancing their right to defend themselves with the necessity of law to defend everyone. The progress of the Ottawa Landmines Treaty, which has now been signed by two-thirds of the world's governments, is a salutary example.

There are other treaties, the Non-Proliferation Treaty, for instance, that need much more comprehensive support. And it is important for the US, in particular, to realize that it cannot expect to be a credible leader among the nations of the world if it lags behind in fighting our most serious problems, including mines and nuclear weapons, and if the US does not meet its financial obligations in full, on time, and without preconditions where the United Nations is concerned.

As individuals and as nations, we must move from the law of force to the force of law. It is time for all of us, governments and individuals alike, to embrace, extend, and empower the structures for peace created in the last one hundred years. We must invest them with the full legal and moral authority to stop violence before it begins. We must strengthen the mechanisms to resolve differences peacefully and to make their resolution by force ultimately unthinkable by instilling in everyone a culture of peace. This fundamental need was the oxygen behind the global effort in 1998 to create a statute for a permanent International Criminal Court. Citizens of the world must embrace a culture of peace, moving from armaments to agreements, and in so doing necessitate a coming to terms with the thorny issue of security. As long as a nation or a community or an individual feels threatened, violence and recourse to weapons is never far from the surface. But like so much else, the definition of security today is changing.

POSITIVE HUMAN SECURITY FOR ALL

Threats to security today come not only from war, but also from economic and social inequities, human rights abuses, marginalization, and poverty. Over the past decades, my work in Jordan and abroad has been predicated on this premise: that true security is not only a matter of protecting borders from military aggression, but of providing a stable environment for all citizens, women and men of all races and creeds, to participate fully in commercial and political life.

Peace is not merely the absence of hostilities, but a positive human security founded in equity. As King Hussein put it, "What is the real purpose of peace? In our view, it is to promote the security and the prosperity of peoples. Without security, there can be no assured prosperity. And without prosperity, there can be no assured security."

Providing the prosperity that underpins peace requires taking advantage of the new techniques and technologies of globalization. In this boundary-less information age, with productivity becoming ever more divorced from physical resources, the uniqueness of each country's contribution is coming to depend more on the distinctness of cultures and the innovation of individuals. The recent innovations in global communication and commerce are instrumental in bringing the world these unique resources, from the mind-work of computer programmers to the handiwork of craftsmen and women.

For example, the Internet has opened the global market to under-privileged women in Jordan who have been trained by the Noor Al Hussein Foundation (NHF) to produce handicrafts and industrial garments to sustain themselves and their families. Their products are globally accessible through the worldwide website of the NHF, which receives e-mail orders from the US and other markets. This global connection came at an opportune time as the Foundation has been turning over the ownership and management of these income generating projects to the women themselves. Such orders will ensure their long-term sustainability.

The self-esteem and confidence that these women have acquired is as valuable to them as the substantial additional income they earn. In the empowerment of women, especially at the grassroots level, our projects have transformed development thinking in Jordan by moving beyond traditional ineffective social welfare schemes to enable women to become genuine economic and political forces in their communities, thereby increasing their status and influence at every level.

As a result we have seen significant progress in every aspect of quality of life from literacy to family income to population control. These women are building stable, healthy, and prosperous communities, which in turn can engage in regional partnerships in the wider pursuit of peace. These programs, which combine innovation with respect for local values and traditions, have received international recognition as development models for the Middle East and the developing world. Through a network of regional partnerships we are supporting their implementation in other countries. Also, as models for sustainable economic growth and political participation, they have not only reinforced social stability and cohesion in Jordan, they are an essential component of our larger quest for justice, peace, and understanding in the region and abroad.

EDUCATION, A TOOL FOR PEACE BUILDING

World citizens need to be educated, both in the skills required to participate and prosper in the information economy, and, more important, in the skills required for getting along with other citizens of the world. We have seen clearly over the past decades that it is not enough simply to sign a peace treaty. We are very conscious of the importance, if we are to overcome the enmity of previous generations, of encouraging the next generation, the future guardians of peace, to understand both their opportunities in a changing world and their duties towards themselves and others.

Our experience over the past decades has taught me that education is a supremely effective tool for peace-building, especially when it brings together students of differing ideas, backgrounds and even cultures, at a time in their lives when their minds are most open and receptive to programs emphasizing tolerance, cooperation and conflict resolution. It can give them the tools to make their voices heard on issues that affect them. I have seen this process at work in a number of institutions, in Jordan and around the world. For instance, the Jubilee School in Amman, established as a tribute to King Hussein's Silver Jubilee, was originally conceived in 1977 and has now graduated six years of students. It serves promising scholarship students from throughout the region, with special emphasis on less-developed areas of Jordan, promoting community service, creative thinking, information technology, leadership and conflict resolution skills. Our graduates excel at the best US and other international universities, committed to return home to their local communities and to make an extraordinary difference.

The problems that these future leaders will have to address will go beyond politics, economics, or even peace. Being a citizen of the world means realizing that we have a responsibility to the world itself, as well as to its human inhabitants, and to future generations.

As King Hussein said to the United Nations Conference on Environment and Development, "Our goal is to ensure that environmental protection becomes as deeply embedded in our national psyche and in our human spirit as our existing commitments to balanced development, pluralism, human rights, and regional peace based on justice and international law. We are deeply committed to this goal, despite the severe constraints of political, economic and demographic pressures on our country . . . for we would be morally, politically, and perhaps even criminally negligent if we were to place financial profits and material comforts above the goal of the integrity of our earth, the welfare of our people, and the life prospects of our children and grandchildren." I believe that his words best express the responsibilities of being a citizen of the world.

New Understandings of Citizenship: Path to a Peaceful Future?

Elise Boulding

T he world needs loving! Gaia herself, the Commonwealth of Life on the planet, needs loving. So do all six billion humans, in our 10,000 societies[1] spread across 189 countries, with our 2000 languages. The peoples of those ten thousand societies, remarkably enough, gathered together through their representatives well over 50 years ago to declare,

We the Peoples of the United Nations, Determined

to save succeeding generations from the scourge of war, which twice in our lifetime has brought untold sorrow to mankind, and

to reaffirm faith in fundamental human rights, in the dignity and worth of the human person, in the equal rights of men and women and of nations large and small, and

to establish conditions under which justice and respect for the obligations arising from treaties and other sources of international law can be maintained, and

to promote social progress and better standards of life
in larger freedom, . . .

Have Resolved to Combine Our Efforts to Accomplish
These Aims. . . .

The result was the formation of the United Nations, and yes, the
United Nations is part of this world's incredible diversity and needs
loving, too.

The overlay of 190 sets of national boundaries on this world's
diversity has left many ethnic, racial, and cultural identity groups,
each with their own history, stripped of access to their traditional
resources and excluded from opportunities to participate in the new
lifeways of the new states in which they find themselves. Such identity groups include also the diasporas of immigrant communities
and victims of past centuries of slave trade. The resulting struggles,
fueled by a military technology that multiplies the availability of
small arms to angry people and of high-level bombing power to a
few major powers, almost makes the dream of putting an end to
war seem obsolete.

Yet the capacity to vision a world at peace has been part of
humankind's heritage over the millennia, and is with us still. So are
the practical peacemaking skills of the ten thousand societies, present
in memory and tradition but missing in practice because of fast-
moving developments that outstripped possible strategies of adap-
tation. So is the capacity for developing and learning new
peacemaking practices suited to the complexities of this rapidly
changing world. The twentieth century was a century of research
and development of such practices, stimulated by the Hague Peace
Conference of 1899. Today there are peace teams, the contemporary equivalent of Gandhi's Shanti Sena (peace army), at work in
many conflict-torn areas. But too few, and with too few resources.
Military technology has outraced peace technology.

This outracing is the result of another type of heritage: recent
centuries of colonial invasion of many of the territories of the ten
thousand societies and a large-scale drawing of maps that ignored

their own traditional lands. Suddenly there were sovereign states with a ruling group that excluded other ethnic groups within their borders from economic and social opportunities in a world in which everything was changing. Diversity was deplored. Political modernization was all about assimilation and melting pots, but reality was about oppression and exclusion.

Only now, with the twenty-first century threatening ecological, economic and social catastrophes, is there a dawning realization that diversity is valuable, that every language and every lifeway includes some valuable knowledge and skills (as well as undesirable practices, such as clitoridectomy, which are certainly not to be cherished!). UNESCO has played an important role in this realization, especially through its activity in declaring the World Cultural Development Decade (1988-1997),[2] which called the attention of all states to the riches of each other's many cultures. Ethnic groups are finding their voices again, and an increasing number of states, especially in Europe, are following the once-unique Swiss model of a federation of semi-autonomous provinces, each with their own language and culture but also a shared confederal system of governance. Africa, Asia and the Americas all offer examples. On the European continent, the Council of Europe is encouraging this process through the Framework Convention for the Protection of National Minorities adopted in 1995. Scotland and Wales now have their own parliaments in the United Kingdom (the situation in Northern Ireland is still in process), with similar developments in Belgium, Spain, Italy, and Scandinavia.

A New Model of Citizenship

In fact, a new model of citizenship is emerging for the states of the contemporary international community. This citizenship is rooted in love of one's own community, one's own culture, with a deep sense of civic responsibility for its well-being, but extends the feelings of community and civic responsibility to all those who live within the borders of one's country. It resonates to the symbols of citizenship—the flag, the constitution, and the institutions and processes of governance of that country. This is different from the assimilation model of citizenship because it values and respects the sister identity groups within the borders of the country.

However, citizenship that limits its loyalties to those within its borders leaves us with 189 states each focused on maintaining sovereignty in relation to the other 188 states. This passion for sovereignty curbs the willingness of states to sign treaties limiting their freedom of action. And yet behavior-limiting treaties are essential if states are to deal with conflicting interests without going to war. How to create a responsible system of mutually limited governance among sovereign states?

The new model of citizenship that hovers on the horizon is not only multicultural, involving respect for all groups of fellow citizens within the state, but is multinational and multidimensional: a three-fold citizenship. The first dimension, one's local community, has already been emphasized as a part of one's citizenship in the state, which in turn is the second dimension of citizenship. The third dimension of citizenship has yet to be recognized and explored: citizenship in the United Nations itself. The United Nations was formed as an association of "we, the peoples," as quoted at the beginning of this essay, not as "we, the states." I do not mean to make this simply a play on words but, rather, to suggest that all six billion of us humans (and our fellow creatures in the biosphere) have a direct stake in the survival of the United Nations. The willingness of our national representatives to sign treaties to protect the security of all life is dependent on our civic activity in promotion of such treaties.

What weaves the local, national and United Nations dimensions of our citizenship together in a common fabric is the existence of 25,000 international nongovernmental organizations (INGOs). These INGOs bring concerns for peace, justice, human rights, and the environment from our local chapters to the national and on to the United Nations level, with specific access points at the United Nations, including especially the UN conferences and commission hearings on critical world issues. These INGOs are a new development of the twentieth century and are still in a learning mode, particularly in terms of learning how to relate international INGO offices to local situations, to *learn* from locals, and to learn from and cooperate with each other in this still new action sphere of international nongovernmental bodies. This is all part of a wider learning process as the new concept of citizenship evolves.

An important aspect of learning how to exercise that citizenship involves overcoming the vast public ignorance about the United Nations which exists in every country. The concept of national citizenship as encompassing active awareness of the diversity of peoples and needs within our own country already requires a major new educational effort, and the added challenge of learning how to work within the United Nations is daunting, to say the least. But if we want to enable the development of a workable United Nations system of governance to solve the many types of economic, cultural and environmental conflicts already being faced within the international community of states, we have no alternative.

The body of existing conventions and treaties that binds the states of the United Nations together is the product of thousands of hours of citizens' time (in their role as representatives of INGOs) put into continuing dialogue with diplomats and representatives of member states and United Nations officials over the nature of the problem to be solved, and what can be agreed to in the way of solutions that are in the common interest of states with different needs. This process, slow and frustrating as it is, brings into being new norms in the common human interest. The United Nations treaties on the law of the sea, the banning of land mines, and the establishment of the International Criminal Court are all recent achievements of this process.[3]

US RESISTANCE TO INTERNATIONAL TREATIES

The United States, one of the original funding states of the United Nations itself, has in recent years been notably resistant to signing and ratifying many of these treaties, especially regarding arms limitations and the environment. It also withdrew from the United Nations Education, Science and Culture Organization (UNESCO) in the 1980s, in protest over the report of UNESCO's MacBride Commission on the New World Information Order (1980), which emphasized two-way information flows between countries of the North and countries of the South to replace a one-way flow from North to South.

All citizens of the United States must share the blame for this withdrawal because we have not activated our citizenship in the United Nations itself to prevent the withdrawal. How could this be done? A specific opportunity at this time is to become involved in the United Nations Culture of Peace Decade, 2001-2010. Activities associated with this decade are strongly recommended to us by the collective voice of Nobel Peace Laureates. Since the theme is education for peace and nonviolence for the children of the world, educational materials have been developed for kindergarten through high school, for faith groups and community social action groups of all kinds.[4] Peace studies programs to support learning about peacebuilding already exist in many colleges and universities in the United States and around the world and will contribute to the Decade's work. This focus on peace education will not only help develop the skills of listening and dialogue but the skills of civic participation through grassroots organizations and INGOs. Educational materials about the United Nations itself are available directly from the United Nations Association of the United States (UNA-USA)[5] (or from the UNA of any member state).

Imagine how different the world would be if everyone read the quarterly UN Chronicle,[6] which reports on United Nations activities! Invisible as the United Nations is to the general public, there is a lot going on, on any particular day, in the United Nations system. Few realize what that system consists of: six major United Nations operating organs, 13 associated bodies, 16 specialized agencies, five regional commissions, and fluctuating numbers of peacekeeping and observer missions, as well as 20 research institutes, other divisions and special programs which continually evolve to meet new needs in various parts of the world, two United Nations Universities (one in Japan, one in Costa Rica), and about 50 worldwide information centers, plus special offices where new field programs are located. The research institutes publish their own newsletters and research reports. What a difference it could make if all disarmament activists read the reports of the United Nations Institute of Disarmament Research (UNIDIR), or development activists read the reports of the United Nations Research Institute on Social Development (UNRISD), to name just two valuable United Nations research bodies.[7] It is a tragedy that all the creativity and problem-solving activity which goes on in the United Nations, side by side with the more publicized bureaucratic inefficiency, is unknown to most civic activists. So many missed opportunities for support of important peace, human rights, development and environment initiatives that, if carried out, would make the United Nations a more effective body!

RESTORATIVE JUSTICE

In activating the United Nations component of our citizenship, we are supporting principles of restorative justice that have been badly eroded by the evolution of punitive criminal justice systems in recent centuries of state-building. It is a very simplistic system: find the wrongdoers, and punish them. The much older system of restorative justice, still practiced in many tribal groups, though outlawed by colonial occupiers, is far more complex. It involves identifying the wrongdoer, uncovering the circumstances of the wrongdoing and the full extent of the harm done, helping the wrongdoer take responsibility for the harm done, and undertaking some form of restitution for the victim, and to the extent possible restoring relationships, not only between the wrongdoer and the victim but between the wrongdoer and the community. When well-trained United Nations Peacekeepers are stationed in an area recovering from civil war, this is the kind of work that their special cadre of trained conflict mediators will undertake.

Soldiers without special training can only rely on force in areas of unrest. It is a sad fact that United Nations peacekeeping is severely handicapped by a great shortage of soldiers with special peacekeeping and peacebuilding training, and an equally severe shortage of civilian police officers for the UNCIVPOL, the United Nations Civilian Police Force. The good news is that the United Nations Security Council has recently mandated that women be present in significant numbers in all United Nations peacekeeping missions.[8] Here are new career opportunities for the growing number of women entering into professional conflict mediation and conflict transformation work. But funding to support the missions is sadly lacking.

The Culture of Peace Decade could well be a decade of developing understandings of the meaning and possibility of United Nations citizenship for young people. Service in the United Nations Volunteers program gives young people and mid-career people the opportunity to participate in United Nations peacekeeping and development projects around the world (as well as in the national peace corps of member states). Here is a way for young people to learn about the rich diversity of lifeways and languages around the planet, to explore the poetry and music and dance of human life, to thrill to the biodiversity of the rivers, mountains, valleys and oceans, the deserts and the plains—in short, to fall in love with the world that so badly needs loving.

The process that began with the Hague Peace Conference in 1899, when nations assembled to declare that war should no longer be used as a means to settle conflicts between states, is still alive. The twentieth century saw the establishment of the World Court, the League of Nations, and finally the United Nations. The peace research movement brought social scientists together from every discipline to study the processes involved in conflicts and their resolution, and institutes to research and develop peace diplomacy were established on every continent. New professions of mediators and conflict transformation specialists developed. Social movements to end violence in all its forms arose, including the restorative justice movement to end the use of prisons for wrongdoing, and social movements to end all forms of economic and racial/ ethnic oppression.

The United Nations began a long process of slowly crafting treaties that would limit the types of weapons used in war and move toward, first, nuclear disarmament, and then, general and complete disarmament. Most of all, the treaties have aimed to protect civilians, who are increasingly becoming casualties of new military technologies used in war, and of economic catastrophes in the form of slave-type sweatshops. But treaty-crafting is a slow process—states resist having their options limited. And the arms race never stopped—even more lethal military technologies are being developed, and World War II established the practice that it is okay to bomb cities; civilian casualties are just "collateral damage."

MORAL NUMBING

Who can say when the current process of moral numbing—a condition of moral and emotional unresponsiveness to human slaughter—first began? Did it begin with the bombing of Dresden? With the nuclear bombing of Hiroshima and Nagasaki? With the Gulf War? Or more recently with the bombing of Kosovo? Or has it, in fact, been an unnoticed byproduct of Western colonialism, the destruction of native peoples' lifeways and habitat, and the transatlantic slave trade? Is it not strange that a century noted for a growing awareness of human rights marked by the United Nations Declaration of Human Rights should not have brought that moral numbing process to a halt?

The horrified responses in the United States to the September 11 acts of terrorism gave a different kind of witness to that moral numbing. Yes, there were intense feelings of fear and vulnerability, deep sadness over the deaths, but a very rapid translation of those feelings into willingness to fight a vicious war against innocent civilians in the name of stamping out terrorism. The voices calling out in protest, "not in our name," are hard to hear. The media ignores them.

Yet the peacebuilding initiatives of the previous century have not been in vain. There has been a steadily growing realization that cycles of vengeance and counter-vengeance can destroy the societies involved and must be stopped. It is possible to create a social space between vengeance and forgiveness, so that those who have been enemies can learn to live together again. The first step was creating international criminal tribunals, with justice as the primary objective. But gradually the concepts of the restorative justice movement have gained relevance as people consider how conflicting parties, whether tribal, clan-based, different ethnicities, faith communities, or primarily political groups, would be able to give each other room to get on with their lives after fighting stopped. The need to deal with feelings of injury, anger, and the desire for compensation was strong. And so it happened that the governments of some conflict-fractured states, working with grassroots organizations and national as well as transnational NGOs and the United Nations, worked to develop a new type of institution related to older concepts of folk law: the truth commission.

TRUTH COMMISSIONS

The South African Truth and Reconciliation Commission is the best known. The commission process is a long and tortuous one, but there are now between fifteen and twenty states that have established some form of truth commissions. A 1995 study[9] lists truth commission processes in Bolivia, Argentina, Uruguay, Uganda, Philippines, Chile, South Africa, Chad, Rwanda, El Salvador, Guatemala, Nicaragua, Brazil, Colombia, and Peru. They are sparse in Asia, with truth commission initiatives taking place in Sri Lanka and Cambodia, and certainly under consideration elsewhere.

The truth commission process involves an intensive examination of the meanings of citizenship and responsibility of conflicting groups for each other within a given country. How much forgiveness is possible? How much restitution can be made? By whom? How will healing take place? The United Nations has made important contributions to the truth commission process in a number of countries. Many trained helpers are needed in countries where there has been widespread killing and torture. Those involved in the violence must relearn their humanity. UNESCO's Culture of Peace program has worked with local peace centers to help reintegrate into local communities the former soldiers and guerillas who have engaged in widespread torture in countries such as Nicaragua.[10]

Germany is the only European country that has had a commission to assess the consequences of war—in this case, focusing on the period of separation of East and West Germany. There has never been serious public discussion of a Truth Commission for the United States. The nuclear bombing of Hiroshima and Nagasaki, resulting in massive civilian deaths, has never been dealt with. Much of the information about the fate of the citizens of Hiroshima and Nagasaki remains classified to this day. The bombing is rationalized as having speeded the end of the war, although a 1998 study[11] indicates that capitulation was already under way. An effort by the Smithsonian Institute in Washington, DC, to hold a 50th anniversary exhibit about the bombing was simply stopped by government pressure.

Failure to grieve over its own shortcomings is a serious problem for the United States and contributes to anti-American attitudes in the rest of the world. A new movement for United States reparations to African-Americans for the harm done by slavery, and to Native-Americans for harm done by driving them off their lands, may well link with the anti-bombing lobby and peace and disarmament groups to create a demand for a United States Truth and Reconciliation Commission that could lead to public dialogue about the historical process of development in a country justly proud of its democracy, but not well enough aware of its history, and of the diversity of peoples who proudly call themselves Americans. This could give new meaning to American citizenship, as such Truth and Reconciliation Commissions have given new meanings to citizenship in the countries that have worked through that healing process.

A More Inclusive Understanding of Citizenship

I have been suggesting that a more multidimensional and inclusive understanding of citizenship, one that could make a peaceful world possible, has strong emotional components of involvement in one's own local community, in one's own country, and in the United Nations itself. Both the national and the United Nations components of citizenship involve respect for and empathy with the highly diverse Others with whom we share that citizenship, and a sense of identification with the world family, composed of identity groups and ethnicities scattered across 190 states. The United Nations represents us all. Can we love the United Nations flag as much as we love our country's flag?

This is the only planet we have, and the planet itself needs loving if the life it now supports is to continue into the future. And so I will close with a Sonnet by Kenneth Boulding, whose last words before he died in 1993 were, "I love the world."

Sonnet for the Turning Earth[12]
21 January 1993

How good it is to live on Earth that turns,
That endlessly repeats the simple play
That gives us the great plot of night and day,
Sunrise, noontide, and sunset, and so earns
For us the precious skill that learns
To see the patterns in time's brave display
And so prevents our plans from going astray,
So we don't dash into a fire that burns.

Good it is too that Earth goes round the sun
In annual cycles, giving blessed seasons
So that we search successfully for reasons
Even though in some patterns we may see none.
So it is clear that what makes human worth
At least in part is learned from Mother Earth.

1 The 10,000 societies is a term referring to the existence of thousands of ethnicities, and appears in UNESCO's 1996b report on "Our Creative Diversity," as well as in Guy Ankerl's *Coexisting Contemporary Civilizations*. Geneva: INU Press, 2000.

2 See UNESCO, *A Practical Guide to the World Decade for Cultural Development, 1988-1997*. Paris: UNESCO, 1987.

3 A vivid description of citizen's involvement in the development of the law of the sea is found in *Citizen Action for Global Change. The Neptune Group and Law of the Sea*, by Ralph B. and Miriam L. Levering, Syracuse University Press, 1999.

4 See Elise Boulding, *Cultures of Peace: The Hidden Side of History*. Syracuse University Press, 2000, for more information about current developments with regard to peace culture and the involvement of INGOs in peace development work. For specific information about Culture of Peace Decade activities, contact David Adams, Global Movement for a Culture of Peace and Nonviolence, 256 Shore Drive, Branford, CT 06405. On the Internet, *adamslpeace@aol.com*.

5 The UN Association of the United States (UNA-USA) is located at 801 Second Avenue, New York, NY 10017-4706.

6 The United Nations Chronicle is published quarterly by the United Nations Department of Public Information, United Nations, Room DC2-0853, New York, NY 10017.

7 UNDIR and UNRISD are both located in the Palais des Nations, CH 1211, Geneva, Switzerland.

8 The resolution on the importance of women in peacebuilding is Resolution 1325, adopted by the Security Council at its 4213th meeting, on 31 October 2000. Copies are available from International Alert, One Glyn St., London SE11, 5HT, England.

9 See *Transitional Justice: How Emerging Democracies Reckon with Former Regimes. General Considerations*. Vol. I, N. Kritz, ed., Washington, DC: U.S. Institute of Peace. See also Martha Minow's *Between Vengeance and Forgiveness, Facing History After Genocide and Mass Violence*. Boston: Beacon, 1998.

10 An example of that type of healing program is found in Z. Narvaez, ed., *Promotores de Paz, Revista del Prorama de Educacion y Accion para La Paz*. Vol. 2, Numero 1, Februero 1997. Managua, Nicaragua, Centro de Estudios Internacionales.

11 See K. Bird and L. Lifschutz, eds., *Hiroshima's Shadow, Writings on the Denial of History and the Smithsonian Controversy*. Stony Creek, CT: The Pamphleteers Press, 1998.

12 See Kenneth Boulding, *SONNETS FROM LATER LIFE, 1981 - 1993*. Pendle Hill Publications, Wallingford, PA, 1994. The sonnet is on page 55.

Reviving the Dream of Global Democracy

BY RICHARD FALK AND ANDREW STRAUSS

The 1990s brought great hope to humanity: the peaceful end to the Cold War and to apartheid, the liberation of East Europe, sustained economic growth in many of the poorest regions of the world, steps toward holding political leaders responsible for crimes of state, the spread of democracy and human rights, the strengthening of regional institutions, especially in Europe, the emergence of global civil society as a real political force, the impact of social action designed to make globalization more equitable and environmentally protective, and robust coalitions of governments and civil society actors that completed projects such as a treaty prohibiting anti-personnel landmines and an agreement to establish an international criminal court. Without exaggeration, a normative revolution was underway that if sustained, would result in "a new world order" based on humane global governance, and of benefit to all peoples on the planet.

Of course, all was not well. There was much violence and turmoil in the world, and bloody civil wars raged in several parts of sub-Saharan Africa and the Balkans. The United States did not exert leadership in world affairs during the years following the collapse of the Soviet Union to move toward nuclear disarmament or to establish an independent peacekeeping force under the authority of the United Nations. And "the peace process" that was supposed to end the Israel/Palestine encounter turned out to be a failure. Globalization also ran into some speed bumps in the form of the Asian

Financial Crisis, as well as a rising tide of protest and a series of emergencies arising from countries such as Turkey, Argentina, and Indonesia on the brink of bankruptcy and chaos.

And yet, overall, these problems seemed manageable with wisdom and patience.

Then came the terror attacks of September 11, and an American response that opted for global war, starting in Afghanistan, but dedicated to a long struggle on many fronts with the visionary goal of eliminating the terrorist dimension from international life. It has seemed that the power of the United States was such that it could reshape the global agenda overnight, making its campaign against terrorism dominate all other issues, and as in the Cold War, put on indefinite hold projects for global reform. Whether such control will be successfully maintained is difficult to discern at this point, but it will depend on the degree to which citizens associations and grassroots initiatives rise to the challenge, and recover the momentum that had been gathering so impressively in the 1990s. There are some early encouraging signs: it appears that an International Criminal Court will exist before the end of 2002, the World Social Forum in Porto Allegre, Brazil was the largest meeting ever of citizens from around the world seeking an alternative globalization, and there appears to be growing support for the establishment of a fully sovereign Palestinian state that shares Jerusalem as its capital.

A GLOBAL PEOPLES' ASSEMBLY

In this essay, we explore another test case: whether the social forces around the world can carry forward the vision of global democracy, and more specifically, whether a start can be made during this decade on a vital component of this vision, the creation of a Global Peoples' Assembly (GPA) or parliament. It seems essential to have such an institutional presence for the expression of ideas, grievances, and proposals that are not acceptable to leading governments, but are needed for the wellbeing of the peoples of the world. The practicality of this initiative has been demonstrated in Europe where the European Parliament has gradually and fitfully grown from a neglected talk shop to becoming an integral dimension of European political life, and a key counterweight to concerns that popular sentiments and societal values were being stifled by the Eurocrats in Brussels. The European experience provides a model of constitutional structure and of process, whereby an innovative institution learns, adapts, and continuously reinvents itself.

The justification for global democracy relates to the new ways in which global policy is being made, and the degree to which non-territorial networks are undermining the authority and control of territorial actors. The dark side of networking is evident in relation to terrorism, drugs, crime, illegal migration, financial speculation, and environmental decay. But networking has its brighter sides, as well, with the Internet and information technologies generally, providing peoples with extraordinary instruments of empowerment. It enlarges the possibilities of participation, awareness, and accountability by many orders of magnitude. In fundamental respects, the push for global democracy is to give political shape to these developments, both to resist the dangers associated with globalization-from-above, including unbridled corporate and financial control of the world economy and the prospects of the militarization of space, as well as to move ahead with the opportunities associated with globalization-from-below, especially reviving the normative revolution of the 1990s. The aspirations for global democracy will only remain credible if concrete steps are taken to give these widely shared sentiments some sort of institutional presence. For this reason alone the project to establish a GPA in the coming years deserves a high priority from activists around the world.

Such a priority is also needed to overcome some resistance to democratizing moves that had been earlier underway. One of the exciting developments during the 1990s was the extent to which representatives of civil society were active participants at global conferences on big issues such as environment, human rights, women's issues, and social development that worked in collaboration with more progressive governments to exert influence on the positions taken by the assembled governments. The very success of this informal experiment in global democracy produced a kind of backlash, leading some states, particularly Russia, China and the United States, to mount criticism of such events as wastes of time and money, mere "spectacles." As a result, the UN can no longer integrate civil society actors into its main consciousness-raising activities.

NEW FORMS OF PARTICIPATION ARE NEEDED

It was a notable additional contribution of the United Nations to give credibility to the idea that the Organization needed to incorporate into its activities both representatives of civil society and of the private sector. Kofi Annan, during his distinguished tenure as Secretary General, has frequently given eloquent expression to this view that governmental representation is no longer enough to ensure the continued relevance of the United Nations. In a world of transnational activism and networking, new forms of participation must be found. The Secretary General took the lead, despite some resistance from prominent member states, in sponsoring a Millennial Assembly of Civil Society on a one-time basis to make a contribution to the various observances of the year 2000.

It is an open question of feasibility and effectiveness whether to work for the establishment of a GPA as a second assembly within the framework of the United Nations or as a free-standing institutional presence. The advantage of the latter approach is that it can begin to happen as soon as enough funding and political support is forthcoming. There have been various recognitions of the relevance of the GPA idea that can be viewed as seedlings. Steps have been taken by individuals and groups in several countries to establish shortly an e-parliament that would engage in debate and produce proposals entirely online. Another creative development has been the biennial Assembly of the United Nations of Peoples held in Perugia, Italy on four separate occasions, bringing together representatives from over 100 countries to discuss common concerns over a period of several days. The Perugia events, as does the Porto Allegre Social Development Forum, show clearly that the voices of the peoples of the world are giving expression to a range of different demands, dreams, and proposals that come to the surface in inter-governmental organizations.

Against this background of thought and action, it seems possible to highlight this project to establish a functioning GPA within the next several years. There are many obstacles and challenges that make the task seem formidable, but as has been often suggested in such circumstances, even the longest journey begins with the first steps. It will be important to take these steps to rekindle the hopes of peoples around the world that the September 11 attacks not be allowed to put on hold the various dimensions of global reform, and more specifically, the importance of globalizing democratic practices and procedures in a manner that takes account of globalizing trends with respect to the organization of the world economy and international security.

Military globalization, led by the United States, with its plans for missile defense and the weaponization of space, its distrust of arms control arrangements, its unilateralism, makes this effort to build an effective global democratic presence of urgency. We can expect the poor and most vulnerable peoples on the planet to be particularly threatened by this prospect of American ambitions to control the earth as a whole on the basis of its dominance in military might. A consensus for demilitarization, for nuclear disarmament, for peace and justice needs to be shaped to offer alternative concepts of human security and of a world dedicated to the use of its resources to meet the needs of people rather than the greed of markets and the geopolitical ambitions of rich and powerful states.

Of course, the GPA need not be, and likely would not be, anti-statist, although it would almost certainly be critical of dominant economic and security policies being currently pursued by leading states, and of the misallocation of resources to bolster the military. Indeed, it would likely build on the impressive collaborative experience in the 1990s when coalitions of Non-Governmental Organizations (NGOs) joined with like-minded governments to promote a common agenda that was seeking to get policy results in relation to war/peace, environment, and human rights concerns.

THE PATH TO A GLOBAL PEOPLES' ASSEMBLY

The choice of method for the pursuit of the project of a GPA is of great tactical relevance at this stage. The most conventional approach would be to form a coalition of NGOs around the world that would seek to influence governments to hold a conference at which a treaty of establishment would be tabled for signature and subsequent ratification. The treaty could specify that the GPA would start to function when 30 governments had deposited an instrument of ratification with the UN, and had contributed an assessed amount need for a startup budget. An alternative approach would be to seek voluntary contributions, a founding civil society convention perhaps linked to a meeting of the World Social Forum, and an informal process of establishment based on annual sessions of the GPA held in various parts of the world, or located in either Geneva or New York for maximum impact on the UN system and the world media.

Whatever path is pursued, the founders could delimit the functions and powers of the GPA. If established outside the UN and without the formal participation of states, then it would emerge as a project of global civil society, which would take on the task of building the structures for global democracy. If states and the UN participated, then the GPA would operate within the formal framework of world order, and its innovative status would be viewed as a less radical type of global reform. In either event, the growth of influence and legitimacy would depend on the support that the GPA could gain for its early efforts, and how it conceived of its role, whether as a citizens' dimension of the existing structure or as a transformative platform from which to work for humane global governance, including nuclear disarmament, war prevention, and a comprehensive functioning rule of law.

In any event, the movement for the establishment of a GPA would link peoples throughout the world in efforts to establish the key institutional component of an emergent global democracy. The process would itself be a manifestation of the democratic spirit, a learning experience of political value, and a contribution to defining and supporting the idea of "global democracy." As such, it would provide activists everywhere with a hopeful focus for their grievances, and a practical means by which to work for peaceful change and social justice in the difficult years ahead.

A Renunciation of Nuclear Weapons, One Citizen at a Time

By Dennis Rivers

A Citizen's Renunciation of Nuclear Weapons

Mindful of the extreme dangers and costs that nuclear weapons bring both to the world and to those who rely on them, and mindful of America's practical, moral and spiritual need to serve life rather than build instruments of death,
I, Dennis Rivers,
a citizen of the United States of America,
renounce, withdraw my citizen's consent for, and oppose any design, production, testing, planning for use, or use of nuclear weapons by the United States, against any nation, group, persons or person, at any time, and under any circumstances. I declare to my elected representatives and to all agencies of the United States government that if I die in an act of mass murder against the United States, I do not want further acts of mass murder committed in my name. I make this declaration in my own name and in the name of Saint Francis of Assisi and all the children of the future.

Signed this 14th day of April, in the year 2002:

Dennis Rivers
Resident of Santa Barbara, California

Rabbi Abraham Joshua Heschel, one of the most inspiring and beloved Jewish teachers of the twentieth century, was also a regular participant in protests against racial segregation and the war in Vietnam. Asked once about the slim chances of actually influencing the course of events, he replied that when we protest, we do so not only to achieve certain results, but also to save our own souls. The Citizen's Renunciation of Nuclear Weapons (and the related documents on the www.nonukes.org web site) evolved out of my efforts to face my own responsibilities in regard to the nuclear weapons of my country, the United States, and to save my own heart from the silent death of numbness and denial. For these weapons, in effect, belong to me. They have been created to defend me, and they have been created with my tax dollars and the assumption of my consent. My silence on this matter gradually becomes my consent to be "defended" in this way. I have decided to issue my own citizen's renunciation of the use of nuclear weapons under any circumstances, and to encourage others to do the same. This may seem like an extreme position. Here are the considerations that have driven me to it.

I have been jolted into this renewed protest by President Bush's announcement that the United States intends to use nuclear weapons not only to deter nuclear attacks, *but to deter and respond to any attack or even threat of attack*. This represents an enormous widening of the scope of possible nuclear wars, regardless of the much-announced current plans to reduce the total number of nuclear bombs held by the United States and Russia. Official pronouncements that this has been U.S. policy for some time do not lessen the danger of a dangerous path.

TEACHING BY EXAMPLE

One major problem with threatening to use nuclear weapons is that we have to be very ready to carry out that threat. That means we lose any moral credibility in trying to control the spread of nuclear weapons, or to persuade our opponents to negotiate rather than escalate. Unfortunately, when people make threats, they actually instruct and invite those threatened to make the same threats back. For half a century the United States has been asserting its will in world politics backed up by the threat of nuclear weapons. Now, every maniac on the planet wants to get his hands on one. I can't help thinking to myself, as an American: What lesson about power did we think we were teaching the world all those years?

And President Bush, like his predecessors of both parties, still does not seem to understand this process or that people watch what we do. By threatening to use nuclear weapons in a wider and wider range of circumstances, he is telling everyone how useful they are. More countries will make them, and they will get easier and easier to steal. (How confident are you that Pakistan can safeguard its nuclear weapons?) Eventually someone who hates us will get one and use it on us. Or we will end up living in a computerized security state in order to try to avoid that fate. Or we will have to carry out our threat and then have to cope with new waves of hatred against us. We have no way of knowing what our threats will provoke.

A balance of terror, or the threat of retaliation, can never bring us security. As the September 11th attacks on America demonstrate so tragically, overwhelming force will not keep us safe in a world where more than a billion people are angry, hungry, and hopeless. If we want to be safe, it seems to me, we need to invest our resources in making a world that offers a better life for everyone. Instead, we are being invited to invest more and more heavily in the machinery of destruction. Since 1940 the United States has spent approximately six *trillion* dollars on nuclear weapons. (That is about $1,000 for every man, woman and child now living on planet Earth!) And this investment is a seductive, addictive, and self-aggravating process. First there were the tremendously expensive airplanes and missiles to deliver them, and now we are told we need to invest in expensive new missiles to shoot down other nations' missiles.

GROWING RESENTMENT

Meanwhile, when we spend new hundreds of billions on military hardware, we do not spend those billions on schools and hospitals around the world. The global gap between the rich and the poor grows worse, resentment against America grows, we become more endangered and more in need, according to our experts, of new bombs and missiles. Some nations come to oppose us, like Iran or Libya, and I think because we imagine we could obliterate them with nuclear weapons if we chose, we do not really work very hard at healing the divisions in the world. Now, like gamblers who can't stand to face the money they have lost, our political leaders can't stand to face that our six trillion dollars spent on nuclear weapons has bought us only a world full of hatred, fear, poverty, and violence.

I have come to believe that our own misplaced faith in weapons, our blindness to human needs, and our contemptuous dismissal of those whose guns are not as big as our guns, will be our undoing, more than any foreign enemy. This is one of many the reasons why I have decided to say No to the use of nuclear weapons on my behalf under any circumstances. Nuclear weapons are worsening the problems they were supposed to solve.

There are other serious problems with the mere possession of nuclear weapons, even before anybody uses them. One of them is that a person's character is defined not just by deeds after the fact, but largely by what a person is willing to do, plans to do, and will refrain from doing. If I am willing to infect a city with smallpox, or release nerve gas in a subway, and I plan to do so, I am morally depraved as a person, even if I have not gotten around to actually performing those actions. With a heavy heart I must confess that I have become convinced the same holds true for our planning to use nuclear weapons.

Nuclear weapons make it impossible to protect civilians from injury and death, as required by the Nuremberg Principles and any normal person's sense of restraint. Nuclear weapons explosions release massive amounts of radioactive poisons, which rain down on thousands of square miles of the surrounding land, cities, towns and people. Our readiness to use them is thus, God help us, our readiness to commit mass murder and poisoning. What is left of our character after that? This is another of the many reasons why I have decided to say no to the use of nuclear weapons on my behalf under any circumstances.

The moral issue just described points to the public side of character. There is also the subjective side of life. How do I feel about being alive? How do I feel about being me? How do I feel about people planning to commit mass murder on my behalf? If I have qualms of conscience, I am sure that I can blot them out of awareness with sufficient quantities of drugs, alcohol, and/or violent entertainment. Or perhaps just get very buried in my work, buried enough that I don't feel much about the world around me. The question is, what is left of my life after I do that?

What Can an Ordinary Citizen Do?

So, what is an ordinary citizen to do? Nuclear weapons programs began in secrecy and continue to this day to be shrouded in secrecy and far from citizen influence. And yet, as citizens in a democracy, we have an open-ended responsibility for all that is done in our names. It occurred to me that one beginning step I could take to fulfill that responsibility would be to very publicly *withdraw my consent* from this process, and to do this in a way that is consistent with the seriousness of the issue. Hence the statement at the beginning of this article and a longer one on the www.nonukes.org web site. I intend to send copies to the president, my senators, my representative, newspaper editors, TV news directors, and so on. Several of my friends plan to take similar steps and to give copies to their children with instructions to pass these documents on to future generations of their families.

Nuclear illnesses and mountains of nuclear waste will travel down to the generations after us. It may be comforting to people in the future to know that at least some people in this generation opposed nuclear weapons and the genetic mutations they bring. This is what ecopsychologist Joanna Macy calls "deep time," holding all future generations in our hearts today. At every step along the way I am trying to follow Gandhi's advice and "be the change I want to see." With regard to nuclear weapons that means trying to embody the caring and thoughtfulness that I would like public officials to bring to the nuclear issue.

I may not individually be able to stop the United States from its nuclear folly, but I can at least stand up and tell public officials not to invoke my name as a justification for it. And in my longer version of the Renunciation statement, which I invite you to read on the www.nonukes.org web site, I say more about the changes that would make this ever-smaller world of ours a better world to live in than the one we've got now.

I am clearly trying to change the course of events, and yes, I am trying to save my own soul, too; trying to hang on to some personal integrity as a citizen of a country that publicly denounces weapons of mass destruction while secretly planning to use them in expanding ways. Perhaps if many people take this personal responsibility for what is being done in their name, the soul of our world might be saved.

I know one thing for sure. If I die in a mass murder attack on the United States, I do not want additional mass murders committed in my name. Someone, somewhere must say *stop, turn, turn toward life, turn away from the instruments of death*. I invite you to study, reflect, pray, and join me in making such a statement.

The Earth Charter:
A Blueprint for Peace and Citizen Action

By David Krieger

The Earth Charter is a blueprint for peace. It represents the hopes and dreams of millions of people for our common future. It is built upon an understanding of our shared humanity and our inextricable link with the web of all life. It is premised on our shared responsibility for passing the world on intact to the next generation and the next and the next. We must not be the generation that breaks faith with life and with the future.

Never before in human history has the danger to our survival been greater. Today we live in a world in which nations are pitted against nations, in which wars are commonplace, in which overwhelmingly the victims of wars are civilians, and in which terrorists strike out at innocent civilians. All of this must change if we are to survive, if we are to flourish, and if we are to realize our full potential as human beings.

The Earth Charter is a call to action. It is a call to all of us to rise to our full potential as human beings and to play our part in changing the world. Without our actions, the Earth Charter is only a flowery document—words upon a piece of paper. It is up to us, by our actions, to breathe life into this vision of global decency.

Our Human Gifts

Each of us is more special than we can possibly imagine. We are, in fact, miracles of creation. Each of us is entirely unique. There has

147

never been anyone quite like you—with your combination of interests and talents, knowledge and appreciations—in the entire history of the universe. But beyond our magnificent uniqueness and our diversity, we all share a common humanity.

We have been endowed with gifts that we often fail to realize or to use.

We have the gift of thought and reflection, allowing us to grapple with the world's problems and to find creative solutions, such as the Earth Charter itself.

We have the gift of memory, making it possible for us to learn from our mistakes and those of others.

We have the gift of voice and language, enabling us to communicate and to make our voices heard.

We have the gift of conscience, enabling us to determine for ourselves right from wrong.

We have the gift of creativity, allowing us to add to the world's already enormous store of beauty through art and literature, philosophy and religion, science and engineering, and day-to-day problem solving.

We have the gift of love, making it possible to share closely with others the incredible gift of life in all its richness and beauty as well as in its sorrow and suffering.

We have the gift of empathy, allowing us to understand another's hurt and sorrow and to reach out with compassion and love.

We have the gift of mobility, making it possible for us to go where we are needed.

We have the gift to make and use tools, enabling us to extend our powers dramatically.

Our tools have taken us into outer space, where our astronauts and cosmonauts have looked back on our beautiful, blue planet, so alone in the universe, so precious in its nurturing of life.

And our tools have given us the power to destroy ourselves. That is the essence of the Nuclear Age. We can no longer be assured that the continuous flow of life, at least human life, will continue.

Our tools are dual-purpose because we are dual-purpose, creatures capable of both good and evil.

The Choice is Ours

And we must choose. Choice itself is another of our great gifts as human beings. We each have the power of choice that we manifest each day of our lives by every action we take and by each decision we make.

I believe that we are more powerful than our tools, including our most terrible weapons of mass destruction. We have the power to control these tools and to eliminate them. But we must exercise that power or our tools may eliminate us.

As the Earth Charter tells us, the choice is ours: "We stand at a critical moment in Earth's history, a time when humanity must choose its future."

That choice can be made by our apathy, complacency and ignorance. That is the choice of abandoning our humanity by default. That is the choice of abandoning our human responsibility. It is the choice of those who would sleepwalk through the greatest challenges of our time, perhaps of any time.

That choice can be made by giving over our power to leaders who would lead us into war and greed and selfishness. That is the choice of abandoning our democratic responsibilities and playing the role of lemmings rushing over a cliff to our demise.

Or our choice can be made by standing on our own two feet, by embracing others, by our compassion, our creativity and our commitment to changing the world.

To choose the path of peace and decency will not be easy. In fact, it will require every ounce of courage that we have. We will have to learn to believe in ourselves and to empower ourselves to be a force for peace, even against great odds.

We will have to stand firm and confident in the power of right and decency against entrenched and powerful institutions that would have us be complacent consumers rather than active peacemakers.

Standing for Peace

At the dawn of the Nuclear Age, just days after the first atomic weapon was dropped on the city of Hiroshima, Albert Camus, the great French writer said, "Before the terrifying prospects now available to humanity, we see even more clearly that peace is the only battle worth waging. This is no longer a prayer but a demand to be made by all peoples to their governments—a demand to choose definitively between hell and reason."

Let us stand with Camus and choose peace, because it is necessary. Let us stand with Camus and demand that our governments choose reason.

War no longer has a place on our planet, and we must stop preparing for war. We must stop squandering our resources on tools of destruction. We must demand that the $850 billion now being spent on the world's military forces be spent instead on meeting human needs. If human needs are met and principles of justice among all peoples are adhered to, there will be no need for war, and the need for defense will atrophy.

Martin Luther King, Jr. said, "One day we must come to see that peace is not the distant goal we seek, but the means to that goal."

Let us stand with Martin Luther King, Jr. and choose peace because it is a wiser course of action, respectful of human life. Let us join him in his dream for justice and dignity for all. Let us stand with him in his conviction that peace and nonviolence are not only the ends we seek, but also the means to attain those ends.

Eleanor Roosevelt said, "The future belongs to those who believe in the beauty of their dreams."

Let us stand with Eleanor Roosevelt and believe firmly in the beauty of our dreams. Let us believe deeply that the vision of the Earth Charter is not only right and necessary, but also possible. It is not an idle dream, but a vision of a world that must be built by our actions.

Pablo Casals, the great master of the cello, said, "The love of country is a splendid thing. But why should love stop at the border?"

Let us stand with Pablo Casals, and choose to be citizens of the world. Let us erase the borders in our minds and replace them with an all-embracing love for humanity. Let us work to create a world in which every person, no matter where he or she is born, is able to live with dignity and full human rights as set forth in the Universal Declaration of Human Rights.

Jacques Cousteau, who explored and shared the beauty of the oceans and who lived with a deep commitment to future generations, said, "The time has come when speaking is not enough, applauding is not enough. We have to act."

Let us stand with Jacques Cousteau and commit ourselves to action—to action that will change the world, even if it is done one person and one decision at a time.

The Dalai Lama has reminded us that we must never give up. He has written: "Work for peace. . . . Never give up. No matter what is going on around you, never give up."

Let us stand with the Dalai Lama, who has spoken so passionately for peace and nonviolence, and pledge to never give up our struggle for a more decent and peaceful world, a world we can be proud to pass on to the next generation.

The human future stands on soft and precarious ground. Looking ahead, one path leads to war and devastation. Another path, far more hopeful, is the path of peace. But it must be an active, energetic and organized peace. We cannot wait for peace to come to us. We must choose peace and commit ourselves to attaining peace by our actions. A starting point for doing so is saying NO to war.

THREE STEPS FOR PEACE

I would like to ask each of you to take three steps to help build a peaceful world and make the Earth Charter the reality we live by.

First, say NO to nuclear weapons—all nuclear weapons—no matter who possesses them. You can go to the Nuclear Age Peace Foundation's web site at www.wagingpeace.org and sign our Appeal to End the Nuclear Weapons Threat to Humanity and All Life. While you are at the web site, you can sign up to receive our Sunflower e-newsletter that will keep you informed monthly about the latest developments in working for a nuclear weapons-free world.

Second, say NO to war. Write to your elected representatives today, and tell them that war is an unacceptable alternative and that they must find peaceful means through the United Nations and international law to resolve conflicts. Send more letters to your newspapers and talk about this with your friends. You can find a sample letter and contact information at the Waging Peace web site.

Third, say YES to peace and choose hope. Put aside complacency and despair and choose hope as the basis for all of your actions from this day forward. Not frivolous hope, but hope that is rooted in courage, compassion and commitment. Stand up for peace, for human dignity and for future generations in all you say and do.

The Earth Charter states, "As never before in history, common destiny beckons us to seek a new beginning." Let us begin.

hope

VOICES OF YOUTH

Light and Love: The Only Weapons We Need

By Hafsat Abiola

(Hafsat delivered the following speech upon receiving the Nuclear Age Peace Foundation's Distinguished Peace Leadership Award in November 2001.)

Thank you very, very much for this honor. Indeed, this honor is for my parents, because without my parents I would never have started the work to bring democracy to Nigeria. Nigeria is a country in West Africa that was for many years ruled by the military system. From the time I was born in 1974 until my twenties, we had only a few years of democracy in Nigeria, so I knew very little about democracy. We had democracy when I was four years old until I was nine. I don't really remember that time at all, but in my teens, my parents sent me to the United States to finish high school. It was in the United States that I started to see the new system. In Nigeria, we had soldiers tell us what to do, and because they had guns, we could not tell them differently. If we did tell them differently, we were harassed. If we were not harassed, we were put in prison. In a worst-case scenario, you could get killed. That was all I knew when I was growing up.

When I came to the United States, I found a country where, if you spoke to your government, your government listened to you. If you attacked your government, your government explained to you. If you challenged your government, your government explained. If you wanted, you could vote them out of office, if you felt they had not performed well enough. We could never vote our military leaders out of office in Nigeria. After some time, the military leaders began abusing our people, and stealing all the country's money and putting it into private bank accounts.

In 1983, my country was a middle-income country. Today, it is one of the poorest countries in the world. Our average income is $240 per capita, and that is how Nigerian people live from day to day. If they are sick, they cannot go to the hospital to get medicine. Even if they can go to the hospital to get medicine, they cannot afford to buy food, because they must use this money for the medicine. There are four hours of electricity in Nigeria each day. There are 100,000 telephone lines for 120 million people. I can't explain to you how deeply Nigeria is in poverty. It is not because we do not have resources. Nigeria has an abundance of wealth. It is because our government was never listening to its people, and it did not care about our welfare. In fact, this is the only way of life Nigerian people have ever known. When Nigeria was created in the 1800s, it was created to serve England, and all our wealth served the British. When we gained our independence, our wealth served the soldiers.

MY FATHER BECOMES PRESIDENT AND IS IMPRISONED

For some reason in 1993, the Nigerian military decided that they wanted to have a democratic election. In fact, it was the young people in Nigeria who forced them to do so. The young people on Nigerian University campuses read books, and saw that all countries were not like Nigeria. They saw that there were other countries where there was democracy and where there was freedom. So the young people began challenging the government, saying, "You're not doing a good job, it's time to go." Finally, the government said Nigeria would have elections, and my father won the presidential election. However, the military decided after the election that they really were not ready for democracy. They put my father in prison, in solitary confinement.

My mom, a high school graduate and a mother of seven children, decided that, out of love for her husband, she would start to work and speak out against the military. And she did. Somehow the people in my country listened to her, and moved beyond their fear and began organizing themselves to protest. They had sit-in strikes and demonstrations. The market women gathered, and would close down their shops, even though they knew that they needed to sell in order to eat. They did all of this, which took so many personal sacrifices. Thousands were put in jail, thousands were killed, but they did all of this because they wanted a chance to govern themselves. As the Nigerian military saw that my mother would not stop organizing the people of my country, they assassinated my mom.

I was a sophomore student at Harvard University when my father won the election. I was in my senior year in 1996 when my mom was killed. During this time, I did nothing because I did not know what to do. I was frightened; I wanted my father home. I wanted the military to stop tapping the phones of my home, and tailing and harassing my mother. I really didn't know what to do. I knew I was in one of the greatest democracies in the world, but I thought that American people didn't care. Oil companies that were U.S. companies and British companies were giving the military money every year in Nigeria. The Shell Company was giving the military weapons, which they were using to kill people. So, as far as I knew, the Western countries did not care about my people. But American young people taught me differently.

AN IMPORTANT LESSON

I was walking past Widener Library at Harvard University when I saw a table of young American kids. They were just the kind of kids that I really didn't pay attention to in school. They had long, long, long, long hair, or they had spiked hair that was really spiked and short and purple, or spiked and short and green. It looked very greasy, as if it hadn't been washed in a while. I was looking forward to avoiding those students. When I saw them, I wondered what were they petitioning for, because I could tell they were petitioning. I thought to myself, "What are they petitioning for now, the right to walk barefoot on campus? How truly revolutionary!" I was looking for a way to avoid them. But somehow, I think they sensed that I was trying to avoid them, and they came up to me. They said, "We're getting signatures, there's an elected president in prison in Nigeria, and we're trying to fight for his freedom." I was so moved that day.

I said to them, "Do you know that you're talking about my father?" And they didn't know that. They said, "Well, we really don't know what's going on, but Amnesty International sent us some information. Could you come and tell us what's going on?" I went and I told them, and that was the beginning of our movement around the world to free Nigeria. Those young students at Harvard University helped me build a movement. We got our University campus to help us by engaging in talks with Shell, because Harvard has stocks in Shell.

There is an elementary school called Martin Luther King Elementary School, and the students there brought me to speak to them. The students were seven years old, and I really don't think they understood a word of what I said. But, after I came to their school, their teacher told them to write down something about this young lady who came, and I took all the things that they wrote. The young students marched from their school to the City Council of Cambridge and they said they wanted to help Nigeria. I remember I was there that day, little kids, probably no more than up to my thigh, had written down on a piece of paper that they wanted to help Nigeria. They sat down and told the City Council, "My name is Allison, and this woman is from Nigeria...." Council members started crying. I wasn't sure what they were saying, but, it didn't seem to matter, because the Council members started crying immediately. They were all just so open. When I finally told the Council members what was going on in Nigeria, they didn't just look at me as, "Who is this, and what does Nigeria have to do with us here in America?" They had heard from their youngest voices and these voices told them that somehow this was important. So the Council members listened to me.

We did this all across the United States, and got millions of people engaged in trying to fight for freedom in Nigeria. As the voices had been silenced in Nigeria, the voices of the American people, especially America's youth, rose up to replace them, and amplified them until the whole world was listening. In America, in Canada, in Europe, in Asia, the Commonwealth, the United Nations, and everyone finally started talking about freedom in Nigeria.

KUDIRAT INITIATIVE FOR DEMOCRACY

I built an organization soon after my mom was killed. I named it for my mom. I called it the Kudirat Initiative for Democracy. It was meant to work with young people and women to help us build democracy across the continent of Africa. Again, young people across the United States and across the world helped me. We heard that five to ten million young girls around the world have been sold into sexual slavery in foreign countries, and we started a movement to help them. We heard that HIV/AIDS is killing two million people in Africa every year, and we started HIV/AIDS workshops across the continent to help them. We heard that unemployment was a big problem across the world, and especially in the developing world, with sixty percent unemployment, especially among young people, in Africa. We started a project to generate five hundred million new jobs for young people across the world.

We couldn't be stopped, and we can't be stopped. We intend to make this world the most beautiful, glorious planet that any human being can imagine, and really, beyond anything any human being can imagine.

In 1998, with the work of young people fighting for freedom in Nigeria, the military saw the writing on the wall. They started a set of elections that ended nine months later, with us having our first democratically elected president in Nigeria in May 1999.

Nigeria remains one of the poorest countries in the world, but if you were to come and visit me there, you wouldn't know it. There is such dignity in the people now. We feel like our troubles are our own problems, and we can solve them together. We feel like we're engaged in the world, trying to make an experiment in Nigeria that the world can be proud of, knowing that the democracy that we have in the Nigeria was midwifed by people across the world that have never even been to Nigeria. There is such pride and such dignity in our people now. When you come, their love and joy just embraces you. I would invite you all to come and witness that. I invite you to understand another thing. When we were asking for democracy in Nigeria, the normal US foreign policy pattern said it was more important to be concerned about economic interests in another country than in those issues because those issues get too complicated anyway. The young people in America said that should not be so. We must follow our deepest ideals.

When September 11th happened, and the World Trade Center was attacked, one of the first presidents to call President Bush was my president, President Obasanjo. He said that we are really sorry about what happened. Then he came to meet your president. He came as an emissary following a meeting of all Africa's leaders. They sat down to look at what they could do to offer assistance. They said, well, we can offer our army, and we can offer any other kind of support but the United States needs to let us know. Our president came with this message to deliver to President Bush: *We are really sorry about what happened; please tell us how we can help.*

When President Obasanjo came, you wouldn't have known that he came from a country that has barely enough to take care of its own people. But now that we have a democracy, we have all that we need to move forward. We have all that we need to be engaged as responsible citizens of the planet. President Obasanjo came as an emissary of the 120 million people in Nigeria, and as an emissary of the people of Africa to ask you how we can help, to stand with you now in what is perhaps the greatest threat that the world has ever faced.

SPEAKING TO THE ADULTS

I want to speak now to the adult people in this room. I want to say to you that we are so deeply grateful for your honoring me as a young person, and honoring Craig Kielburger. We're so deeply grateful for your work that you've carried with such integrity to make this world so much better—to make it nuclear-free, to eradicate poverty, to take care of HIV/AIDS, to take care of all of the evils on the planet. I want to say that I completely understand that this honor is not so much because of the things I may have done, as impressive as it might seem to you, but because of what you would like us to do, because of the potential that young people have, and that I know you see in us.

It is also because you understand that you cannot do this work all by yourselves and you need us to join with you. I am so deeply honored to accept that beautiful, gracious, kind, generous invitation. I can think of no better way to live my life than to act in the service of all humankind and all of life. I really look forward to you giving us challenges, and telling us to do more, and doing still more, until all of the things that we don't like on the planet have been addressed and transformed.

SPEAKING TO THE YOUTH

To the young people, I know that you've come in here thinking that you've come to recognize two young people. But you've really come in here to recognize yourselves. You made the difference for me and for all the people in my country, and you will make the difference for the world.

You might be thinking of losing ten pounds. You might be thinking of graduating with an A+. Whatever you may be thinking of accomplishing to show that you have something to make you feel like you are worthy, I want you to know that you're already worthy. You are already enough. You're already all that we've been waiting for. You have such light in you. I have been to your college campuses and your high schools, and I have to say that you are beautiful and generous, and there is such a clear glowing light in each of you. Guard your light and protect it. Move it forward into the world and be fully confident that if we connect light to light to light, and join the lights together of the one billion young people in our world today, we will be enough to set our whole planet aglow.

I want to give you a poem to hold you on that journey. It's a prayer that was given to my angel mother Lynne by a reverend, following the World Trade Center attacks and it says,

> There are only two feelings in the world, love and fear.
>
> There are only two languages, love and fear.
>
> There are only two acts, love and fear.
>
> Two motives, two procedures, two frameworks, two results,
>
> Love and fear, love and fear.

I want share a lesson that I learned from Lynne with all of you. Hatred is not the opposite of love; it is the absence of love. Darkness is not the opposite of light; it is the absence of light. If we would only light our one candle, it would banish all of the darkness. If we would only express our one pure expression of love, we would overwhelm all of the hatred.

YOU ARE NOT PERMITTED TO STOP

To young people and to the adults in the room, you are not required to finish the work, but you're not permitted to stop. So take your light and take your love into the world as the only weapons that we need to make this world truly glorious, truly beautiful, and astonish all of life.

Every Child Is a Treasure

By Craig Kielburger

(Craig delivered this speech upon receiving the Nuclear Age Peace Foundation's Distinguished Peace Leadership Award in November 2001.)

T hank you to the Nuclear Age Peace Foundation for this great honor and for being a visionary organization that recognizes and supports the efforts of young people as peacebuilders.

Tonight, at the 18th Annual Evening for Peace, the Nuclear Age Peace Foundation decided to recognize the achievements of young people. The truth is that we're simply following in the footsteps of organizations and groups like the Nuclear Age Peace Foundation.

Groups like KIND, Hafsat's organization, and our organization, Kids Can Free the Children, realize that we're merely a heartbeat in the history of social justice movements. For example, tonight is the 18th Annual Evening for Peace; I sat there realizing, wow, I was born eighteen years ago! But, the sad reality is that during those eighteen years, there was never a time in which it was so important or so urgent, in fact, to gather together for a united cause—the reason why we're here tonight.

PEACE CARRIES A NEW MEANING

In our post-September 11th world, the word peace carries an entirely different meaning for my generation. This is the first time that we've ever actually experienced war. Conflicts have always been fought far off, in some distant country. We've never actually had, in my generation, a Vietnam, or a Martin Luther King, Jr. or a

John F. Kennedy. The fact is now in our post-September 11th world, even the most politically disinterested young people realize that they cannot ignore what is happening, even halfway around the globe.

Over the past six years, I've had the chance to travel the world, to visit about forty countries, meeting with street children and working with war-affected children. In Palestine, I had the chance to visit the refugee camps and to see how up to sixty people live, sleeping side by side, cramped together, in each tent. I have seen situations where there were no jobs for the men, and very little hope amongst the women and the children. These situations breed anger and frustration.

If we lived in Israel today, for most of the young people here tonight including myself, we would be enlisted in the army. When I was in Israel earlier this year, I met with elementary and middle school students who spoke of the horrors of war in their country. You heard from Hafsat about the situation in Africa, which is even worse in many cases. There are refugees who live literally in sub-human conditions. Children have become acceptable targets of war. In fact, actually, just recently we shipped medical supplies including forty wheelchairs to Sierra Leone, because the Revolutionary United Front, the rebel group there, mutilates—cuts off the hands and feet of women, children and men—as a fear tactic to gain support.

In Northern Ireland, I have had the chance to meet with teenagers who worked as spies and as runners in the current conflict. I have spoken with children as young as twelve years old who left their villages to go into the mountains to join the rebels to fight. Three hundred thousand child soldiers every single day pick up guns because they have no other option to survive.

Children of War

I will never forget visiting Belgrade and Serbia during a halt in the NATO-led bombings, and meeting with a thirteen-year-old boy, who had lived in refugee camps in Bosnia, in Kosovo, and in Serbia. His entire life, he knew nothing except war. When I met him, I asked him what he wanted to do when he grew up. He did not have an answer; he was silent. To encourage him, I tried to explain how I wanted to be a doctor when I was older. He stopped and was silent. Then he said, "You know what would be nice? If we didn't need the doctors anymore because the bombs wouldn't fall in the first place." He was only thirteen years old.

The most extraordinary part of these war-affected children is that they're a source of amazing inspiration because of their courage, because of their indomitable spirit. Their stories never make the front pages of newspapers and never end up on the evening news, but these children are real heroes. These are children who have an indomitable spirit like Anne Frank. They are children who have courage like the students who led the Warsaw ghetto uprising in World War II, children with a spirit of hope, like Sadako.

Sadako was a young Japanese girl. When she was two years old, the bomb fell on Hiroshima. When she was ten years older, she developed leukemia. Following a Japanese tradition that if you fold a thousand paper cranes, you will be granted a wish, Sadako began folding paper cranes to be well again. She died before achieving that dream, but fellow students folded the rest of the paper cranes for her. Her story inspired people around the world to action. Last year, I had the chance to visit Japan and meet with students and educators and to travel to Hiroshima. The most amazing experience was standing there, watching hundreds and hundreds of young people lined up to place paper cranes at the base of the statue erected in Sadako's memory. These children folded paper cranes to symbolize their wish and prayer for peace in the world.

Around the world, the reality for most of these children is there is very little hope. However, young people, whether they be child soldiers in Sudan, whether they be children affected by war in Colombia, whether they be children anywhere around the world, continue to hold onto that dream for hope. And that dream is spreading.

THE POWER OF DREAMS

As young people we are often called naive dreamers for hoping that one day, there will be a world without war, without suffering.

The truth is, it was the dreamers who thought that one day we would end the slave trade. It was dreamers who fought so that the Berlin Wall would fall. It was dreamers who struggled to end apartheid in South Africa. Just imagine if all the young people who are with us here, all the university students, all the high school students, became involved in a single action to promote peace. Just imagine the power that we would have. Or imagine if young people, coast to coast, across the United States, all became involved under one banner, for a single action, united in a cause, promoting peace. We would be unstoppable.

I know that some people here may say that's simply a dream. I know that some of the students here may say that it's hard enough to even organize a school to rally around a spirit week, never mind organizing young people coast to coast across the United States under a single banner, for a single cause. That is exactly what has been happening over the past two months. Young people across the United States, young people in fact around the world, following September 11, were united in their grief, in their compassion, and also in their action.

I was in New York City on September 11th. I was amazed to see the number of young people volunteering in the hospitals, in the blood clinics, and collecting supplies for the rescue workers. Young people in Kids Can Free the Children as far away as Australia sent letters and cards of sympathy to families, and now youth across North America are collecting basic need kits for children in the refugee camps of Pakistan and Uzbekistan.

Kids Can Free the Children

Over the past six years, Kids Can Free the Children grew from a group of twelve-year-olds into what is now the world's largest organization of children helping children. We have over one hundred thousand members in thirty-five nations. We believe that if you are to achieve true peace in this world, you have to work to alleviate the absolute poverty that exists in so many parts of this planet. You have to work to promote education, not only to create greater tolerance, but also to create an embracing of different cultures, different nationalities and different ideas.

This year alone, it is estimated that the world will spend over a trillion dollars on the military. It would only take one-hundredth of that amount, ten billion dollars, to put every single child in the world into school. But where the adults fail, the children meet the challenge. Young people, through bake sales, car washes, and collecting their birthday money, have come together and have raised money to build over three hundred Kids Can Free the Children primary schools in the developing world, providing education to over 15,000 children every day in 21 countries. Children have raised money to build medical clinics, cooperatives, and alternative income projects, especially for women. In the alternative income projects, cows, land, and sewing machines are given to families so that they can actually earn an income and do not have to send their children to the military or to labor in hazardous conditions, and instead can send them to school.

Recently I was in Ecuador, visiting our projects for the opening of three new primary schools. I had the chance to meet with a young boy there named Justo, who is thirteen years old. When he was three years old, his father died. A few years later, his mother fell very ill and was bedridden. He had to take care of his two younger sisters at the age of eight. His dream was to go to school. Not only was this an impossible dream because he was poor, but it was impossible because he was indigenous. In Ecuador, they do not build schools for the indigenous Quechua-speaking population, only for the Spanish-speaking population. About five years ago, a group of students who knew of our work fundraised and built one of the first ever Kids Can Free the Children primary schools, which was in Justo's community. When I had the chance to meet Justo, he explained to me how he went to school, how he is now in high school, and how his dream is to become a lawyer and one day fight for education for all children in his country.

One of the greatest developments over this past year is the fact that United Nations Secretary General Kofi Annan, and Under-Secretary General Olara Otunnu, came to Kids Can Free the Children with a unique challenge. They asked us to be a lead organization for the *International Decade for a Culture of Peace and Non-Violence for the Children of the World*. With the Nuclear Age Peace Foundation, we are working to empower young people by teaching them about the horrors of war and horrors of nuclear weapons. We are also teaching them and empowering them with conflict resolution skills. Our sister organization, Leaders Today, hosts trainings, literally across the United States and around the world. In fact, the Foundation's Youth Outreach Coordinator, Michael Coffey, came with us last summer to Kenya. He joined us on one of our volunteer trips on which we take young people to Kenya, Nicaragua, India, Jamaica and Thailand to build bridges with young people by volunteering and learning about other cultures and traditions.

I'm excited to say that tomorrow, the Nuclear Age Peace Foundation is sponsoring us to work with forty young people here in Santa Barbara. We are holding an event to empower young leaders here so that they can become ambassadors for peace. We are also partnering with the Foundation in a project to build a hundred schools in post-conflict nations and we are shipping medical supplies to meet the needs of children. One of the most exciting things we are doing is a project called "War is Not a Game" for young people here in the United States. In exchange for handing in their toy war guns during Christmas and Hanukkah, the money raised will be sent to Kids Can Free the Children. In turn, we will set up a scholarship fund to buy real guns from ex-child soldiers and give them a chance to go to school. The reason I share this with you is not just so you know about what we are doing, but as a challenge to the young people here to show what youth are capable of, to become ambassadors for peace and to become positive changemakers.

THE FUTURE IS WITH THE CHILDREN

As I close, I want to share with you an experience that I had during my recent trip to Ecuador. We were in the indigenous communities and were fortunate enough to take part in an age-old tradition called the *minga*. It is a tradition in which all the neighboring villages put aside their differences and they come together for a united goal, a united cause, to work as one to help all. Men and women, children and elders from three villages all walked to one community, where they worked in the pounding sun all day to hoist and place the roof on a Kids Can Free the Children school. While they were working side by side, they were not receiving money. They were not receiving any personal gain. The reason those villages came together was because they shared a united belief that the future lies in that of their children, a future which they all share.

When we were up in these incredibly isolated communities, that haven't changed in the past hundreds of years, they had never heard of the attack on America. They had never heard of the war in Afghanistan. But I'm sure that they would share with us a message, that whether a child is born in New York City or Kabul, whether a child is born in Santa Barbara or Quito, they are the children of the world and it is our future which we all share. Every child is a treasure. Every child has the potential to be the next Mother Theresa or Nelson Mandela. Every child has the potential to be the next Desmond Tutu or Martin Luther King, Jr.

I want to leave you with a final thought, a quote from one of my heroes, Mahatma Gandhi. He said, "If we are to achieve true peace in this world, it must begin with the children."

A New Generation of Peacebuilders

By Marc Kielburger

A s I sit in front of my computer screen preparing to write an article on my hopes for the future, my mind begins to imagine a new world. I think of countless possibilities if the next generation of politicians, business people, social scientists, parents, educators, and students were to work together for common goals and objectives. As a young person, my generation is inheriting a planet with a myriad of problems: holes in the ozone layer, regional famines, widespread human rights abuses, and the exploitation of children around the world, to name just a few. My generation is also living in a society in which world leaders are often more concerned about their re-election and the preservation of their political power than leaving a positive and lasting impact on humankind.

GROWING UP IN THE MIDST OF INCREASING VIOLENCE

One of the most pressing challenges which I feel as a young person is having to live in a world marked with ever increasing strife and violence. The end of the Cold War may have decreased the threat of some forms of violence, such as proxy wars. However, it has unleashed new disputes onto the world stage. It is clear that the emergence of internal conflicts is increasing in number and intensity. Nations such as Afghanistan, Angola, Sri Lanka, Rwanda, Kosovo, and East Timor have been besieged by intrastate strife with devastating consequences. As a result, an entire generation in these states has grown up in the midst of ethnic and religious rivalries, or contests over governance and power.

According to the United Nations, one–half of the 48 countries which it defines as "least-developed" have experienced conflict in recent years. The United Nations High Commissioner for Refugees (UNHCR), moreover, estimated that in 1995, some twenty-seven million people were forced from their homes, many of them fleeing from internal strife, causing them to seek sanctuary elsewhere. After personally visiting Algeria, Bosnia and, most recently, Serbia, I have witnessed firsthand the horrific effects of war and how these nations, especially their young people, have been left spiritually, morally, and physically crippled. I have seen and met young children who, instead of toting their school backpacks, carry an AK-47.

The rules of war do not seem to apply in the emerging internal conflicts, as the raping of women, torturing of prisoners, and killing of children are all too common. These wars are no longer between governments, which have the ability to dictate the rules of procedure. The parties pitted against each other are now, more than ever, peoples who have ethnic, cultural or religious differences which are often deeply rooted. Thus, even with the enactment and acceptance of humanitarian international law, there have been massive human rights violations and attempted genocides in this past decade alone, in the case, for example, of Rwanda and Bosnia. As history has witnessed, the reaction of the world community to these internal conflicts has been minimal.

As a student at Harvard University, I was introduced to Samuel Huntington's theories relating to the causes of civil strife. In his book, *Clash of Civilizations*, Huntington argues that the world is divided into regional groupings based on ethnic lines. Moreover, he states that due to the conflictual nature of these ethnic groups, wars are inevitable in regions where these groups meet. I, however, believe that Huntington is mistaken in his hypothesis. It is my conviction that wars are not inevitable and peace can be achieved, partly by investing time, energy and resources in the young people of countries that have experienced strife, in order to help develop a new generation of peacebuilders.

My Vision for the Future

My vision for the future is simple. It is critical to invest in young people, in order to give them the tools to meet the challenges ahead and to promote a new generation of peacebuilders capable of making significant changes to improve the world. It is possible to break the cycle of conflict through the promotion of peace, cooperation, and understanding among young people. Children growing up in an environment of tolerance, respect, and open communication serve as one of the most effective deterrents for war. It is not enough to solely invest money in peacekeeping, which is often only a band-aid solution, after a conflict has erupted, claiming the lives of thousands of innocent individuals. Children must be taught conflict mediation skills and leadership qualities, and have the opportunity to voice their opinions and concerns in a constructive environment.

Moreover, by strengthening the role of non-governmental organizations and civic society, such groups can help young people work towards the promotion of peace. Through my work with the Nuclear Age Peace Foundation, I have seen first-hand the power that a citizen-based organization can have to achieve and promote understanding and peace on a global level. The Foundation, furthermore, has a Youth Advisory Council and provides programs and information for young people on how to create greater awareness of the issue of nuclear abolition, and how youth, themselves, can become active participants in a world that promotes peace. One of the most important roles of the Foundation is to educate young people about the dangerous threats that are created in a world with nuclear weapons and incessant conflicts. Once more people, especially youth, become aware of how they can become involved in the issue of peacebuilding, the sooner positive change will come about.

Everyone Must Do Their Part

I also believe that everyone must do their part to help achieve a world free from conflict. It is for this reason that I am currently raising funds to build a peace center in Bosnia, on donated land, which will allow Serb, Muslim, Croat, and Gypsy children to come together and learn conflict mediation skills, break down social barriers and become "ambassadors of peace." It is this type of program, which is traditionally overlooked by the United Nations and other international organizations, which, I believe, will create and instill peace in a country that has undergone so much suffering. It is necessary that individuals, governments, and civic organizations begin to look "outside the box" and find innovative ways to promote a sustainable peace.

Many believe that I am idealistic. I am actually shamelessly idealistic. I believe that youth have the power to change the world. When young people, the future generation of politicians and leaders in civic society, have programs and opportunities to create bonds of friendship and establish means of cooperation, they can lay the foundation for future peace.

Teaching Peace: Nonviolence 101

By Leah Wells

C onversations pertaining to work often begin like this:
"What do you do?"
"I'm a high school teacher."
"What do you teach?"
"Peacemaking."
"Huh?"

And then it takes a moment to register. The follow-up question usually is, "Is that a real class in high school?" And thus begins the story of how classes on nonviolence wind up in high schools.

TEACHING THE POWER OF NONVIOLENCE

I tell people about the various chapters, how we start out at the beginning of the semester with personal peacemaking and nonviolent responses to assault. Students always want to know how a pacifist would respond if he or she were to be attacked by a random stranger leaping from the bushes or from behind a dumpster in a dark alley. So I ask them how many of them have ever been physically hit by a random stranger in any way at any point in their lives. Maybe one or two people. Then I ask them how many people have ever been physically hit by a member of their family or someone they know at any point in their lives. Nearly every hand goes up.

We worry about the boogeyman and abandoned buildings but fail to address some of the most conflict-ridden arenas, the places where we usually go—like home, school, and work.

That's how the semester begins, by examining our own personal lives. This first chapter introduces students to nonviolence, the myths, the truths and the power of responding with nonviolent force in our precarious lives. We create a working definition of peace, of violence, of conflict, and of nonviolence. We explore where we need to create spaces for peace in our lives, in our communities, in our state, in our nation, and in our world. We start to learn about consensus, following a process, and taking turns. We begin to disarm our disbeliefs, our doubts, and our misgivings about peacemaking. We start to let our defenses down in order to let peace in.

After establishing a baseline for conceptualizing nonviolence, the class learns about historical figures who usually get the short end of the stick in traditional high school classes. Primary sources are a must in Solutions to Violence, the name of the course which I teach and which my mentor, Colman McCarthy, founded. We study Gandhi in his own words. We watch *A Force More Powerful*, the video series by York & Ackerman which aired on PBS in October 2000. We read Dr. King in his own words, and learn about the civil rights movement, hassle lines, and nonviolence trainings. The class begins to understand the structure and discipline which nonviolence requires. We then read Dorothy Day, learning about intentional communities and communal living. The students I teach are accustomed to mass marketing, consumerism and capitalism, so Dorothy Day's commitment to generosity, hospitality, and precariousness tends to shock them. That chapter demonstrates a very exciting learning curve.

Next we read Gene Sharp, Tolstoy's "Patriotism or Peace," Daniel Berrigan, and a very articulate piece by Joan Baez, which examines a dialogue between a pacifist and a skeptic. We learn about the humanitarian crisis in Iraq as a result of the economic embargo, about the School of the Americas Watch movement, about Cesar Chavez and the United Farm Workers, about sweatshops and maquiladoras, about child labor and child soldiers, about economics and the Pentagon, and about the environment and animal rights. By the end of the semester, the students in Solutions to Violence know how to find alternative news and pacifist perspectives on the Internet from websites like Commondreams, Indymedia, and the Nonviolence Web.

What Students Really Learn

"This class made a difference in my life. I see things in a whole new way now that I didn't see before. I'm not saying this class changed my whole viewpoint on life, but it did help me to be a little more open-minded. I'm seeing a little more color these days than just black and white. I don't think this class is about learning a bunch of stats and info. It's more than that. I've learned to be a little more positive than negative. I hope that the class becomes required in the future."

I hope that my students learn the specifics of nonviolence, that they learn to tell the stories of nonviolence, and that they grow in their understanding of key nonviolent figures both past and present. Even more than the facts, though, I hope that they learn about themselves. About halfway through the semester, I ask the class what they think my goals are in teaching Solutions to Violence. Items from the following list invariably arise each semester in their responses to that question:

Compassion. Compassion is a difficult skill to teach. Everywhere around them in the world, they learn to be tough, not to show their softer side, and that kindness is a weakness. Perhaps the best place to start is teaching with compassion. My mentor, Colman McCarthy, gave me some good advice about how to do this. He told me that before every class, he reminds himself to listen more than talk. He says that good listeners have many friends and poor listeners have many acquaintances. Many people like to talk just to hear their heads rattle. The skill of being a good listener is perhaps the most important one in the teaching profession.

I have learned many things from my students just by listening. In fact, even if I just show up to class and don't say a word, the students will create their own dialogue because they so often need a forum to vent their emotions and share their experiences. When we study Gandhi and review the nine steps for conflict transformation, "Work on your listening skills" is one of the toughest on the list. I ask my class if, when they're having a conversation or argument, they are truly digesting the words of the other person, or if they're planning in their heads what to say next, letting the other person's words go in one ear and out the other. We so desperately want to be heard and understood, but have little experience in truly listening with patient hearts.

Compassion also comes from empathy. I always hope for my students that they make other people's experiences a part of their own, whether they live in the same town or around the globe.

Ownership of their learning. Students have very little opportunity to exercise their natural creativity in school due, in no small part, to the reliance on standardized testing and multiple-choice exams. These brain-numbing techniques lull the students into a passive state of receiving information without truly testing the measure of its worth, without examining it for relevance and truthfulness. Standardized tests stratify students into categories that teachers, administrators, and colleges are comfortable with, but have little bearing on what students have actually learned.

I am interested in students learning. I want them to assume responsibility for their own education, and become partners with the school and their teachers in an active pursuit of knowledge. In Solutions to Violence, students have the opportunity to grade themselves, and each semester they report that this is the toughest assignment. The class writes about what they are learning, how they are learning, and how it is affecting them in their daily lives. Then they must assign a comparable grade so that the administration is satisfied. Learning ought to be a cooperative process. Sharing power with the students shows respect and attentiveness to their autonomy and gives them the opportunity to demonstrate what they have learned. It is also a tremendously valuable insight for me to know what parts of the curriculum reach the students and what elements of truth they have gleaned from the stories, videos and discussions.

This semester, one student said the following: "Why can't you just give us grades, Miss Wells? I mean, if you gave us grades then we could just be angry with you if we didn't like them. If we give ourselves grades, we have to live with what we have done and either be angry or happy with our own effort. Can't you just do our grades for us?" For me, this says it all.

Students are too removed from the processes by which we measure them. Perhaps we don't trust them to give honest evaluations of their work. Perhaps it ought to be part of the teacher's job to evaluate the students independently. But I believe that empowering students to grade themselves is one of the best privileges to bestow on them. They must assume responsibility this way.

Occasionally, students will respond with less-than-honest recommendations for their grades. So we review what they have written as a part of their evaluation, and use their overestimated grade as a jumping-off point. What I have realized all too often, though, when a student grades himself or herself higher than I would have, is that I have not accurately measured what that student has learned, and upon closer inspection, I learn that indeed that student has assumed a great deal of responsibility for taking back his/her education. Sometimes it takes a while to know what you know, though, and test-centered accountability does not take into account this gestation period for knowledge to develop.

Knowledge about the world. Most students do not read the news section of the newspaper. Many students read the sports section, but that is just not comparable. Solutions to Violence teaches them how to dissect the newspaper, learn about the places in the stories, and try to connect with the lives of those impacted by international events. We talk about letters to the editor, discuss news items, and read through articles, point to places on the map and follow up with case studies about places that interest the students, like Palestine and South Africa.

TOOLS TO TAKE ACTION

But Solutions to Violence is about more than just encouraging students to be more informed. It is giving them the tools to take action and create change in their lives, in their school, in their community and in their world.

In the past few semesters that I have been teaching in California, my students have incorporated their theoretical knowledge about how and why nonviolence works into practical action to address current needs in the community and in the world. For example, in response to learning about the mushroom workers' struggles to win a contract for fair pay, better health and retirement benefits, the students organized a school-wide canned food drive to benefit the farm-workers. This particular action impressed me because it was during the last week of school and coordinated primarily by the seniors in the class, people who had tuned out of nearly every other subject and had their minds only on graduation.

Nonviolence is not only about changing the world. Students begin to learn about how their hearts and minds can be transformed by considering peacemaking a legitimate skill. We read a selection from Thich Nhat Hanh's book *Peace is Every Step*, learning to be mindful of our breathing and to recover ourselves and refocus when our attention turns to anger and potential violence. Many times my students have reported that in a tense situation, one where they were ready to lose their cool, they remembered the conscious breathing exercises we do in class, concentrating on naming our in-breath and out-breath. When they were in control of their own emotions through mindful breathing, they felt less likely to react violently. It is this exact personal transformation which makes me believe that Solutions to Violence is a worthwhile class that ought to be a part of any standard high school curriculum.

It teaches them how to be better friends, better children, better students, and better people. It helps them define their talents, articulate their thoughts and cooperate with each other.

I, too, am transformed each semester, impressed with the level of life experience and wisdom my students bring. I learn from them as much as they learn from me.

The Ultimate Goal of Teaching Peace

Teaching peacemaking in school is the most logical non-reactive component to ending intolerance, racism, ageism, and all other forms of personal, structural, and institutional violence. I am hoping that more people will recognize this and that the movement to teach peace will be the saving grace for the sake of our young people, our communities and our world.

WARNINGS AND DREAMS

The Next Hundred Years
Statement by Nobel Laureates

on the occasion of the one-hundredth anniversary of the Nobel Prize

INTRODUCTION

The Statement below was released on December 11, 2001 as 150 Nobel Laureates gathered in Stockholm, Sweden, and Oslo, Norway, for an unprecedented celebration marking the 100th Anniversary of the Nobel Prize. (The prize winners in Physics, Chemistry, Medicine, Literature, and Economics met in Stockholm where their prizes were awarded, and correspondingly, the Peace Prize winners met in Oslo.)

Naturally, the 110 signatories to the attached Statement have their own individual priorities in viewing the future, but all agree to this broad outline of the challenge facing humankind. Among scientists signing are Dr. Francis Crick (Physiology/Medicine, 1962), co-discoverer of the double-helix; Dr. Hans Bethe (Physics, 1967), discoverer of the source of the sun's energy; Dr. Charles Townes (Physics, 1964), co-discoverer of the laser; and Drs. Mario Molina (Chemistry, 1995) and Paul Crutzen (Chemistry, 1995), honored for their studies of the chemistry of the atmosphere and the ozone hole. Among Literature winners are Nadine Gordimer (1991), Günter Grass (1999), and Seamus Heaney (1995), and among Peace Prize winners are Mikhail Gorbachev (1990), Archbishop Desmond Tutu (1984), His Holiness the Dalai Lama (1989), and José Ramos-Horta (1996).

In brief, the Statement warns that the world may explode into war if modern weapons continue to spread and environmental strains remain unchecked. It stresses that we shall not have enduring peace until we address the twin scourges of poverty and oppression, and calls for a new sense of global responsibility.

It hardly need be said that the signatories make no claim to oracular status, but offer their views as a group of concerned citizens.

The following Preamble and Statement were both approved by the 110 signatories.

Preamble

The Statement, prepared in consultation with an extensive group of Nobel prize-winners, was some time in the making. September 11th's appalling terrorist attack occurred after the Statement was written. The terrorization of civilian populations has, for too long, been a horrifying aspect of the global scene. The time has come to end it. This will require a re-shaping of relations within the human family. Our Statement, addressed to the long term, is a plea for just such a re-assessment of our obligations to one another.

Nobel Laureate Statement

The most profound danger to world peace in the coming years will stem not from the irrational acts of states or individuals but from the legitimate demands of the world's dispossessed. Of these poor and disenfranchised, the majority live a marginal existence in equatorial climates. Global warming, not of their making but originating with the wealthy few, will affect their fragile ecologies most. Their situation will be desperate, and manifestly unjust.

It cannot be expected, therefore, that in all cases they will be content to await the beneficence of the rich. If, then, we permit the devastating power of modern weaponry to spread through this combustible human landscape, we invite a conflagration that can engulf both rich and poor. The only hope for the future lies in co-operative international action, legitimized by democracy.

It is time to turn our backs on the unilateral search for security, in which we seek to shelter behind walls. Instead we must persist in the quest for united action to counter both global warming and a weaponized world.

These twin goals will constitute vital components of stability as we move toward the wider degree of social justice that alone gives hope of peace.

Some of the needed legal instruments are already at hand, such as the Anti-Ballistic Missile (ABM) Treaty, the Convention on Climate Change, the Strategic Arms Reduction Treaties (START), and the Comprehensive Test Ban Treaty. As concerned citizens we urge all governments to commit to these goals which constitute steps on the way to the replacement of war by law.

To survive in the world we have transformed we must learn to think in a new way. As never before, the future of each depends on the good of all.

Signatories:
Zhores I. Alferov (Physics, 2000)
Sidney Altman (Chemistry, 1989)
Philip W. Anderson (Physics, 1977)
Oscar Arias Sanchez (Peace, 1987)
J. Georg Bednorz (Physics, 1987)
Bishop Carlos F. X. Belo (Peace, 1996)
Baruj Benacerraf (Physiology/Medicine, 1980)
Hans A. Bethe (Physics, 1967)
Gerd K. Binnig (Physics, 1986)
James W. Black (Physiology/Medicine, 1988)
Guenter Blobel (Physiology/Medicine, 1999)
Nicolaas Bloembergen (Physics, 1981)
Norman E. Borlaug (Peace, 1970)
Paul D. Boyer (Chemistry, 1997)
Bertram N. Brockhouse (Physics, 1994)
Herbert C. Brown (Chemistry, 1979)
Georges Charpak (Physics, 1992)
Claude Cohen-Tannoudji (Physics, 1997)

John W. Cornforth (Chemistry, 1975)
Francis H.C. Crick (Physiology/ Medicine, 1962)
James W. Cronin (Physics, 1980)
Paul J. Crutzen (Chemistry, 1995)
Robert F. Curl (Chemistry, 1996)
His Holiness The Dalai Lama (Peace, 1989)
Johann Deisenhofer (Chemistry, 1988)
Peter C. Doherty (Physiology/Medicine, 1996)
Manfred Eigen (Chemistry, 1967)
Richard R. Ernst (Chemistry, 1991)
Leo Esaki (Physics, 1973)
Edmond H. Fischer (Physiology/Medicine, 1992)
Val L. Fitch (Physics, 1980)
Dario Fo (Literature, 1997)
Robert F. Furchgott (Physiology/Medicine, 1998)
Walter Gilbert (Chemistry, 1980)
Sheldon L. Glashow (Physics, 1979)
Mikhail S. Gorbachev (Peace, 1990)
Nadine Gordimer (Literature, 1991)
Günter Grass (Literature, 1999)
Paul Greengard (Physiology/Medicine, 2000)
Roger Guillemin (Physiology/Medicine, 1977)
Herbert A. Hauptman (Chemistry, 1985)
Seamus Heaney (Literature, 1995)
Dudley R. Herschbach (Chemistry, 1986)
Antony Hewish (Physics, 1974)
Roald Hoffmann (Chemistry, 1981)
Gerardus 't Hooft (Physics, 1999)
David H. Hubel (Physiology/Medicine, 1981)
Robert Huber (Chemistry, 1988)
François Jacob (Physiology/Medicine, 1975)
Brian D. Josephson (Physics, 1973)
Jerome Karle (Chemistry, 1985)
Wolfgang Ketterle (Physics, 2001)
H. Gobind Khorana, (Physiology/Medicine, 1968)
Lawrence R. Klein (Economics, 1980)

Klaus von Klitzing (Physics, 1985)
Aaron Klug (Chemistry, 1982)
Walter Kohn (Chemistry, 1998)
Herbert Kroemer (Physics, 2000)
Harold Kroto (Chemistry, 1996)
Willis E. Lamb (Physics, 1955)
Leon M. Lederman (Physics, 1988)
Yuan T. Lee (Chemistry, 1986)
Jean-Marie Lehn (Chemistry, 1987)
Rita Levi-Montalcini (Physiology/Medicine, 1986)
William N. Lipscomb (Chemistry, 1976)
Alan G. MacDiarmid (Chemistry, 2000)
Máiread Maguire (Peace, 1976)
Daniel L. McFadden (Economics, 2000)
César Milstein (Physiology/Medicine, 1984)
Franco Modigliani (Economics, 1985)
Rudolf L. Moessbauer (Physics, 1961)
Mario J. Molina (Chemistry, 1995)
Ben R. Mottelson (Physics, 1975)
Ferid Murad (Physiology/Medicine, 1998)
Joseph E. Murray (Physiology/Medicine, 1990)
Erwin Neher (Physiology/Medicine, 1991)
Marshall W. Nirenberg (Physiology/Medicine, 1968)
Paul M. Nurse (Physiology/Medicine, 2001)
George E. Palade (Physiology/Medicine, 1974)
Max F. Perutz (Chemistry, 1962)
William D. Phillips (Physics, 1997)
John C. Polanyi (Chemistry, 1986)
Ilya Prigogine (Chemistry, 1977)
José Ramos-Horta (Peace, 1996)
Burton Richter (Physics, 1976)
Heinrich Rohrer (Physics, 1987)
Joseph Rotblat (Peace, 1995)
Carlo Rubbia (Physics, 1984)
Bert Sakmann (Physiology/Medicine, 1991)
Frederick Sanger (Chemistry, 1958; 1980)

José Saramago (Literature, 1998)
J. Robert Schrieffer (Physics, 1972)
Melvin Schwartz (Physics, 1988)
K. Barry Sharpless (Chemistry, 2001)
Richard E. Smalley (Chemistry, 1996)
Jack Steinberger (Physics, 1988)
Joseph E. Stiglitz (Economics, 2001)
Horst L. Stormer (Physics, 1998)
Henry Taube (Chemisry, 1983)
Joseph H. Taylor, Jr. (Physics, 1993)
Susumu Tonegawa (Physiology/Medicine, 1987)
Charles H. Townes (Physics, 1964)
Daniel T. Tsui (Physics, 1998)
Archbishop Desmond M. Tutu (Peace, 1984)
John Vane (Physiology/Medicine, 1982)
John E. Walker (Chemistry, 1997)
Eric F. Wieschaus (Physiology/Medicine, 1982)
Jody Williams (Peace, 1997)
Robert W. Wilson (Physics, 1978)
Ahmed H. Zewail (Chemistry, 1999)

Alfred Nobel's Legacy

By John C. Polanyi

S ome Nobel prizewinners are intelligent. But one hundred of them are no more so. Why, therefore, pay attention to the views of the one hundred who supported the Nobel "Statement," issued to coincide with the 100th anniversary of the Nobel Prize?

The answer is that one's perception of truth comes not from intelligence but from a sense of values. Scholarship embodies those values. Though obscure to many, this was evident to Alfred Nobel, the Swedish tycoon and explosives manufacturer. In his will he stipulated that his prizes recognize *"idealisk riktning"*—idealistic tendencies.

What was it that led to the Nobel prizewinners' Statement? Not a sense of oracular wisdom but of obligation. The thought was present that individuals who had shared the experience of discovery should be able to agree on a great deal more. Nobel was right; science engenders "idealistic tendencies."

But why? Because the pursuit of discovery is shot through with idealism. Discovery originates in the unsupported belief that the book of creation is open to being read. So deep is this idealism that many are willing to devote the best years of their lives to the quest for discovery, though the odds against success are huge.

Idealism must also triumph over the painful fact that the first to read nature's story may well be someone other than oneself. But the truth must be acknowledged whatever the hands that uncover it. Christian truth cannot be elevated over Muslim truth. Nor can accepted truth, backed by the massed armies of orthodoxy, be protected against the claims of upstart facts. One can trace the sense of *noblesse oblige* to these idealistic origins.

What, then, do these hundred voices say? For, despite views to the contrary, the Statement does say something. The initial dissension in the Nobel community testifies to that.

The opening sentence is bold enough to claim that the dominant forces shaping history are rational. This was contentious when written in early July 2001, and appeared still more so following September 11th. The ferocity of the September attack led Americans to believe that the attackers were insane. However, it came to be recognized that the sustained terrorism has its causes and purposes. The question is important, since what lies (to a large extent) within the realm of reason can (to a large extent) be countered by policies grounded in reason.

Of course, the Statement is as much about threats from states as from non-state groups, and about threats of mass destruction as about conventional threats. The dominant setting for conflict in each case, it claims, is a world in which the rich and the poor live in full sight of one another. If in addition the poor are voiceless, they may well be induced to speak through violence, particularly so if their predicament is aggravated by the environmental carelessness of the rich.

It is a peculiar folly, under these circumstances, for the rich to seek greater riches by selling weapons to the poor. Even without this, the prosperous grow ever more vulnerable. Advanced societies are complex and fragile. They operate efficiently by being open, not guarded. Like any complex mechanism, they are, therefore, vulnerable to the wrecker's ball.

To avoid a tragic outcome, the Statement says, we shall be forced to do what we should have done previously. That is to recognize abroad what we have long recognized domestically; the right of all to food, shelter, education, and freedom of expression. This is a revolution in thinking that is already underway. What is lacking, in this country as elsewhere, is a sense of urgency.

Chou En-lai allegedly remarked that it is too early to assess the consequences of the French Revolution. But it is not too early to identify its origins in the willful blindness of the French ruling class of the eighteenth century. Possessed of wealth and power, they offered only promises to the poor.

Unless, in the words of the Statement, we recognize that the future of each depends on the good of all, the coming years will bring escalating conflict. One need not be a rocket scientist to see that. However, the recognition that science has thrived on change could persuade us to behave more like rocket scientists. We might even come to realize that idealism is today the highest form of realism.

A Letter to My Son Luke

By Mairead Corrigan Maguire

D ear Luke,

Today you picked a little yellow rosebud from the garden and carried it into the house to give to me. Your little baby face beamed up at me as you gave me the rosebud. What joy that moment held for me—joy knowing how deeply I love you, and then as I went to put the rose in water, I realized it had no stem, and that without water it would never grow from a rosebud into a beautiful full rose, but that soon, all too soon, it would die.

I felt sad for a moment at this thought and as I watched you toddle across the room, I wondered how I might help you, my little rosebud, grow and "blossom" into manhood. What can I teach you? What can I say to you that will help you to grow up in this "thorny" world, and yet know peace, joy, and happiness, which, dear Luke, are the greatest treasures anyone can possess.

Always know, Luke, that you are deeply loved. You are loved by Daddy and me, and your brothers and sisters. But as you grow up and begin to ask questions for yourself you will know that men and women have a need in their hearts for something more, something deeper than that found even in the very best of human love.

As you walk along the beach at night and listen to the waves lapping gently on the shore, or look up into a night sky at millions of stars, know too that He who created all this, created it for you because He loves you. You are part of this beautiful creation and you are beautiful, special and unique in this Universe. Love, and believe in yourself, because only then can you love and believe in others.

Luke, do not be afraid to love others unselfishly. Yes, many times you will get your fingers pricked on the thorns of disappointment or rejection, but many more times you will pluck the rose of love and receive great happiness and joy from its sweet scent and color. Don't be afraid to risk loving and remember that, as the little rosebud needed the water to live, so much more you and I, and all the people of the world, need to love and be loved. Know that love is the greatest gift you personally can give to another fellow traveler along the "thorny" path of life.

As you grow up in the Christian tradition, struggle each day to be more Christ-like. Pray to be more loving, compassionate, courageous, gentle, and peaceful. Try to see Christ in every man, especially the suffering Christ, and serve and help to remove the causes of that suffering where you can. Remember it is a dead faith that has only words. Acts of love and compassion for the spiritually and materially poorest of the poor is where true faith blossoms.

With ever so gentle steps, walk step-by-step with all the travelers on this "thorny" path of life. They will differ from you in color, creed (there are many paths to God), culture, and politics—but above all remember your fellow travelers have the same needs as you. Our common humanity is far more important than any religious or political ideologies. Treat every man and woman justly and gently as you would have them treat you.

In your life, Luke, pray to be a just man. Your life is precious and sacred, Luke, and your first right as a human being is your right to life. So as you would ask natural justice of your fellow travelers in respecting your right to life, then you too must give justice and respect every person's right to life. This means, my little son, that you must never kill another human being.

It will not be easy for you to refuse to kill. Sadly we live in a world where those who refuse to kill and choose to live nonviolent lives are looked upon as naïve or as cowards. Yes, it will take all of your courage to walk unarmed and to refuse to hate and kill, in a world which insists that you must have enemies and be prepared to kill them before they kill you.

Stand tall and strong, armed only with love, dear Luke, and refuse to hate, refuse to have enemies, refuse to let fear master your life. Only love can bring down the barriers of hate and enmity between people and nations. Hate and weapons only fuel the fear and bring closer the day of war.

Let not one plant in your heart the false seed of pride in any country's flag, a seed that produces the flower of nationalism which grows so wildly, trampling and killing all life around it. Remember always, Luke, people are more important than countries.

I would not give one hair on your precious head for any country—you are more important than any country. And if I feel this passionate love for you, and for my other children, Mark, Joanne, Marie Louise, and John, I too feel passionately for the lives of the little children who are mine too, who today die of starvation in Ethiopia, for the little children in Moscow and the little children in New York who come to believe that they must be enemies and may end up someday killing each other—in the name of the "flag." Remember, Luke, you have no country. The world is your country. You have not only two brothers and two sisters, but millions of brothers and sisters.

Pray also for the gift of wisdom. It is a wise person who soon comes to know that the human family's real enemies are injustice, war, starvation, poverty. But wise people also know that it is only by men and women becoming different and thinking in new ways that these things will become different.

When human life is held as so sacred that no one can kill, then justice will reign in people's hearts and in all lands. Wars will be no more. Justice will mean that no man and woman has too much, while some have nothing. Greed and selfishness will turn into feeding the hungry and removing all poverty. It is possible, Luke, to change this kind of world. You just have to refuse to accept the old ways of thinking and doing things, and begin to think and act in a way more in tune with the magnificent goodness in every man and woman. All men and women know today that killing and starvation is wrong—it is just that not enough are prepared to change themselves and to work on making things different.

And now, my little son, before you fall asleep, let me say the most important thing of all to you. Be happy, be joyous, live every minute of this beautiful gift of life. When suffering comes into your life, and sadly I cannot, much as I would love to, protect you from all suffering, and when you come through the winter of your life, remember that summer will return, the sun will shine again, and the road will be covered in beautiful, oh so very, very beautiful, yellow roses of love.

God bless and keep you, my little Luke.

Mummy

My Dream 3000

By Robert Muller

I dream that we humans,
the most advanced miracle
of life in the universe
will lift our sights, hopes and dreams to the
year 3000
and make the third millennium
a tremendous, unbelievable cosmic success.

I dream that all governments will join their
    minds and hearts
to manage this beautiful Earth and its
    precious humanity
in peace, justice and happiness,

That all religions will join
in a global spirituality,

That all people become
A caring family,

That all scientists will join
in a united, ethical science,
That all corporations will unite
in a global cooperative
to preserve nature and all humanity.

I believe that once and forever,
we will eliminate all wars, violence and
armaments from this miraculous planet.

I dream that the incredible and
growing distance between rich and poor,
between and inside nations
will be eliminated as a blemish
to the miracle of life.
I dream that we will stop the destruction
of our miraculous, so richly endowed
    planetary home.

I dream that we will eliminate all lies,
    corruption and immoral advertisements
    for purely monetary purposes.

I dream that we will all live
simple, frugal lives in order
not to waste unduly the precious resources of our
planet.

I dream that each decade and centennial
will be celebrated as a great
worldwide thanksgiving for our
    successes.

I dream that we will succeed in making
    our planet
the ultimate success of God,

of the mysterious forces of the
universe of which each of us
is a miraculous, cosmic unit.

I dream that the United Nations will
declare a yearly World Thanksgiving Day.

Dear brothers and sisters,
dear children, youth, adults, and elderly,
dear spirits of all the departed,
let us join forces in fulfilling God's
   loving destiny intended for all of
   humanity.

Let us prepare the year 3000
as the most extraordinary celebration
of our grandiose, mysterious journey
in the star-studded heavens.

Let us make this third millennium
a Jubillennium filled with overflowing
   peace, happiness and thanksgiving.

The Message of the Sunflowers: A Magic Symbol of Peace

BY GEORGIANNA MOORE

*Dedicated to the Children of the World
Who Will Sow the Sunflower Seeds of Peace*

O nce upon a time the earth was even more beautiful than it is today. The water was pure and deep, reflecting within itself the sunlight which gave life to all the creatures beneath the waves.

The earth was green with many kinds of trees and plants. These gave food and shelter to the birds, the animals, and to all mankind. At night the air was so clear that the starlight gave a glow almost as bright as the moon.

The people of the earth lived close to nature. They understood it and honored it and never took more than what they needed from it. The people lived in peace, so they prospered and began to build many nations all around the world according to nature's climate.

But one day a terrible thing happened. A strange spirit of greed entered the hearts of mankind. People began to be jealous of one another, and they were not satisfied with all the good things they already had. The nations wanted more and more of everything: more land, more water, more resources. They squeezed precious minerals from the earth to build terrible weapons to defend their nations from other, greedier nations. They killed one another. They polluted the air and the water with poisons. Nature began to die. This is called war. War is ugly. It destroys love and hope and peace.

Then one day a magical thing occurred. The birds of the air, the animals of the land, and the creatures beneath the waters came to an agreement: if they were to survive, something would have to be done to stop these wars. Only through peace could their world survive.

"We cannot speak the human language," they declared, "and mankind can no longer understand ours. We must find among us a symbol of peace so brilliant that all who see it will stop and remember that peace and sharing is beautiful."

"I am what you need," said a golden sunflower. "I am tall and bright. My leaves are food for the animals, my yellow petals can turn plain cloth to gold, my seeds are many and are used for food by all living beings. Yet, the seeds I drop upon the ground can take root and I will grow again and again. I can be your symbol of peace."

All nature rejoiced, and it was decided that the birds would each take one sunflower seed and that they would fly over every nation and plant the seed in the earth as a gift. The seeds took root and grew, and the sunflowers multiplied.

Wherever the sunflowers grew there seemed to be a special golden glow in the air. The people could not ignore such a magical sight.

Soon they began to understand the message of the sunflowers so they decided to destroy all of their terrible weapons and to put an end to the greed and to the fear of war. They chose the sunflower as a symbol of peace and new life for all the world to recognize and understand.

A ceremony was celebrated by planting a whole field of sunflowers. Artists painted pictures of the sunflowers, writers wrote about them, and the people of the world were asked to plant more sunflower seeds as a symbol of remembrance.

All nature rejoiced once more as the golden sunflowers stood tall with their faces turned eastward to the rising sun, then following the sun until it sets in the west.

They gave their goodness to the world so that everyone who sees a sunflower will know that the golden light of peace is beautiful.

* * *

Sunflowers have become the symbol of a world free of nuclear weapons. After Ukraine gave up its last nuclear warhead, the Defense Ministers of the U.S., Russia, and Ukraine met on a former Ukrainian missile base, June 4, 1996. They celebrated by scattering sunflower seeds and planting sunflowers. Former U.S. Secretary of Defense William Perry said, "Sunflowers instead of missiles in the soil would insure peace for future generations."

hope

SOME FINAL THOUGHTS

Unhealed Wounds of Humanity

Auschwitz, Armenia,
Baghdad, Belau, Belfast,
Bethlehem, Bhopal, Biafra,
Bikini, Bosnia,
Cambodia, Chernobyl, Chiapas,
Dachau, Dresden,
Eritrea, Ethiopia,
Guernica,
Hamburg, Hanoi, Hiroshima,
Iwo Jima, Jakarta,
Jenin, Jerusalem,
Kabul, Kandahar, Kashmir,
Kent State, Kosovo, Kuwait,
Manhatten, Midway, My Lai,
Nagasaki, Nanking, Normandy,
Okinawa, Rwanda,
Saigon, San Salvador, Sarajevo,
Sierra Leone, Sudan,
Tibet, Tienamen Square, East Timor,
Three Mile Isand, Tokaimura,
Treblinka,
Wounded Knee, wounded hearts,
And the list goes on. . . .

—David Krieger

On Becoming Human

To be human is to recognize the cultural perspectives that bind us to tribe, sect, religion, or nation, and to rise above them. It is to feel the pain of the dispossessed, the downtrodden, the refugee, the starving child, the slave, the victim.

To be human is to break the ties of cultural conformity and group-think, and to use one's own mind. It is to recognize good and evil, and to choose good. It is to consider with the heart. It is to act with conscience.

To be human is to be courageous. It is to choose the path of compassion. It is to sacrifice for what is just. It is to break the silence. It is to be an unrelenting advocate of human decency and human dignity.

To be human is to breathe with the rhythm of life, and to recognize our kinship with all forms of life. It is to appreciate every drop of water. It is to feel the warmth of the sun, and to marvel at the beauty and expanse of the night sky. It is to stand in awe of who we are and where we live. It is to see the Earth with the eyes of an astronaut.

To be human is to be aware of our dependence upon the whole of the universe, and of the miracle that we are. It is to open our eyes to the simple and extraordinary beauty that is all about us. It is to live with deep respect for the sacred gift of life. It is to love.

To be human is to seek to find ourselves behind our names. It is to explore the depths and boundaries of our existence. It is to learn from those who have preceded us, and act with due concern for those who will follow us.

To be human is to plant the seeds of peace and nurture them. It is to find peace and make peace. It is to help mend the web of life. It is to be a healer of the planet.

To be human is to say an unconditional No to warfare, and particularly to all weapons of mass destruction. It is to take a firm stand against all who profit from warfare and its preparation.

To be human is not always to succeed, but it is always to learn. It is to move forward despite the obstacles.

We are all born with the potential to become fully human. How we choose to live will be the measure of our humanness. Civilization does not assure our civility. Nor does being born into the human species assure our humanity. We must find our own path to becoming human.

—David Krieger

Never Give Up

No matter what is going on
Never give up
Develop the heart
Too much energy in your country
Is spent developing the mind
Instead of the heart
Be compassionate
Not just to your friends
But to everyone
Be compassionate
Work for peace
In your heart and in the world
Work for peace
And I say again
Never give up
No matter what is going on around you
Never give up

—H.H. The XIV Dalai Lama

APPENDICES

Universal Declaration of Human Rights

After a three-year drafting process, the United Nations General Assembly adopted and proclaimed the Universal Declaration of Human Rights on 10 December 1948. The Universal Declaration is the primary international articulation of the fundamental and inalienable rights of all members of the human family. It is the first international statement to use the term "human rights."

Following this historic act the General Assembly called upon all Member countries to publicize the text of the Declaration and "to cause it to be disseminated, displayed, read and expounded principally in schools and other educational institutions, without distinction based on the political status of countries or territories."

Throughout history, men, women and children have given their lives in a long struggle to see these rights and freedoms fully recognized and respected. In that struggle, the adoption of the Universal Declaration of Human Rights represents one of humanity's greatest achievements. Today, the Universal Declaration of Human Rights continues to be the seminal document promoting and fostering human rights worldwide. The Universal Declaration is commemorated each year on Human Rights Day on 10 December. Despite challenges, the Universal Declaration continues to affirm the inherent human dignity and worth of every person in the world.

PREAMBLE

Whereas recognition of the inherent dignity and of the equal and inalienable rights of all members of the human family is the foundation of freedom, justice and peace in the world,

Whereas disregard and contempt for human rights have resulted in barbarous acts which have outraged the conscience of mankind, and the advent of a world in which human beings shall enjoy freedom of speech and belief and freedom from fear and want has been proclaimed as the highest aspiration of the common people,

Whereas it is essential, if man is not to be compelled to have recourse, as a last resort, to rebellion against tyranny and oppression, that human rights should be protected by the rule of law,

Whereas it is essential to promote the development of friendly relations between nations,

' Whereas the peoples of the United Nations have in the Charter reaffirmed their faith in fundamental human rights, in the dignity and worth of the human person and in the equal rights of men and women and have determined to promote social progress and better standards of life in larger freedom,

Whereas Member States have pledged themselves to achieve, in co-operation with the United Nations, the promotion of universal respect for and observance of human rights and fundamental freedoms,

Whereas a common understanding of these rights and freedoms is of the greatest importance for the full realization of this pledge,

Now, Therefore THE GENERAL ASSEMBLY proclaims THIS UNIVERSAL DECLARATION OF HUMAN RIGHTS as a common standard of achievement for all peoples and all nations, to the end that every individual and every organ of society, keeping this Declaration constantly in mind, shall strive by teaching and education to promote respect for these rights and freedoms and by progressive measures, national and international, to secure their universal and effective recognition and observance, both among the peoples of Member States themselves and among the peoples of territories under their jurisdiction.

Article 1

All human beings are born free and equal in dignity and rights. They are endowed with reason and conscience and should act towards one another in a spirit of brotherhood.

Article 2

Everyone is entitled to all the rights and freedoms set forth in this

Declaration, without distinction of any kind, such as race, colour, sex, language, religion, political or other opinion, national or social origin, property, birth or other status. Furthermore, no distinction shall be made on the basis of the political, jurisdictional or international status of the country or territory to which a person belongs, whether it be independent, trust, non-self-governing or under any other limitation of sovereignty.

Article 3

Everyone has the right to life, liberty and security of person.

Article 4

No one shall be held in slavery or servitude; slavery and the slave trade shall be prohibited in all their forms.

Article 5

No one shall be subjected to torture or to cruel, inhuman or degrading treatment or punishment.

Article 6

Everyone has the right to recognition everywhere as a person before the law.

Article 7

All are equal before the law and are entitled without any discrimination to equal protection of the law. All are entitled to equal protection against any discrimination in violation of this Declaration and against any incitement to such discrimination.

Article 8

Everyone has the right to an effective remedy by the competent national tribunals for acts violating the fundamental rights granted him by the constitution or by law.

Article 9

No one shall be subjected to arbitrary arrest, detention or exile.

Article 10

Everyone is entitled in full equality to a fair and public hearing by an independent and impartial tribunal, in the determination of his rights and obligations and of any criminal charge against him.

Article 11

1. Everyone charged with a penal offence has the right to be presumed innocent until proved guilty according to law in a public trial at which he has had all the guarantees necessary for his defense.

2. No one shall be held guilty of any penal offence on account of any act or omission, which did not constitute a penal offence, under national or international law, at the time when it was committed. Nor shall a heavier penalty be imposed than the one that was applicable at the time the penal offence was committed.

Article 12

No one shall be subjected to arbitrary interference with his privacy, family, home or correspondence, nor to attacks upon his honour and reputation. Everyone has the right to the protection of the law against such interference or attacks.

Article 13

1. Everyone has the right to freedom of movement and residence within the borders of each state.

2. Everyone has the right to leave any country, including his own, and to return to his country.

Article 14

1. Everyone has the right to seek and to enjoy in other countries asylum from persecution.

2. This right may not be invoked in the case of prosecutions genuinely arising from non-political crimes or from acts contrary to the purposes and principles of the United Nations.

Article 15

1. Everyone has the right to a nationality.

2. No one shall be arbitrarily deprived of his nationality nor denied the right to change his nationality.

Article 16

1. Men and women of full age, without any limitation due to race, nationality or religion, have the right to marry and to found a family. They are entitled to equal rights as to marriage, during marriage and at its dissolution.

2. Marriage shall be entered into only with the free and full consent of the intending spouses.

3. The family is the natural and fundamental group unit of society and is entitled to protection by society and the State.

Article 17

1. Everyone has the right to own property alone as well as in association with others.

2. No one shall be arbitrarily deprived of his property.

Article 18

Everyone has the right to freedom of thought, conscience and religion; this right includes freedom to change his religion or belief, and freedom, either alone or in community with others and in public or private, to manifest his religion or belief in teaching, practice, worship and observance.

Article 19

Everyone has the right to freedom of opinion and expression; this right includes freedom to hold opinions without interference and to seek, receive and impart information and ideas through any media and regardless of frontiers.

Article 20

1. Everyone has the right to freedom of peaceful assembly and association.

2. No one may be compelled to belong to an association.

Article 21

1. Everyone has the right to take part in the government of his country, directly or through freely chosen representatives.

2. Everyone has the right of equal access to public service in his country.

3. The will of the people shall be the basis of the authority of government; this will shall be expressed in periodic and genuine elections which shall be by universal and equal suffrage and shall be held by secret vote or by equivalent free voting procedures.

Article 22

Everyone, as a member of society, has the right to social security and is entitled to realization, through national effort and international co-operation and in accordance with the organization and resources of each State, of the economic, social and cultural rights indispensable for his dignity and the free development of his personality.

Article 23

1. Everyone has the right to work, to free choice of employment, to just and favourable conditions of work and to protection against unemployment.

2. Everyone, without any discrimination, has the right to equal pay for equal work.

3. Everyone who works has the right to just and favourable remuneration ensuring for himself and his family an existence worthy of human dignity, and supplemented, if necessary, by other means of social protection.

4. Everyone has the right to form and to join trade unions for the protection of his interests.

Article 24

Everyone has the right to rest and leisure, including reasonable limitation of working hours and periodic holidays with pay.

Article 25

1. Everyone has the right to a standard of living adequate for the health and well-being of himself and of his family, including

food, clothing, housing and medical care and necessary social services, and the right to security in the event of unemployment, sickness, disability, widowhood, old age or other lack of livelihood in circumstances beyond his control.

2. Motherhood and childhood are entitled to special care and assistance. All children, whether born in or out of wedlock, shall enjoy the same social protection.

Article 26
1. Everyone has the right to education. Education shall be free, at least in the elementary and fundamental stages. Elementary education shall be compulsory. Technical and professional education shall be made generally available and higher education shall be equally accessible to all on the basis of merit.

2. Education shall be directed to the full development of the human personality and to the strengthening of respect for human rights and fundamental freedoms. It shall promote understanding, tolerance and friendship among all nations, racial or religious groups, and shall further the activities of the United Nations for the maintenance of peace.

3. Parents have a prior right to choose the kind of education that shall be given to their children.

Article 27
1. Everyone has the right freely to participate in the cultural life of the community, to enjoy the arts and to share in scientific advancement and its benefits.

2. Everyone has the right to the protection of the moral and material interests resulting from any scientific, literary or artistic production of which he is the author.

Article 28
Everyone is entitled to a social and international order in which the rights and freedoms set forth in this Declaration can be fully realized.

Article 29

1. Everyone has duties to the community in which alone the free and full development of his personality is possible.

2. In the exercise of his rights and freedoms, everyone shall be subject only to such limitations as are determined by law solely for the purpose of securing due recognition and respect for the rights and freedoms of others and of meeting the just requirements of morality, public order and the general welfare in a democratic society.

3. These rights and freedoms may in no case be exercised contrary to the purposes and principles of the United Nations.

Article 30

Nothing in this Declaration may be interpreted as implying for any State, group or person any right to engage in any activity or to perform any act aimed at the destruction of any of the rights and freedoms set forth herein.

The Declaration of a Global Ethic

This interfaith declaration is the result of a two-year consultation among more than two hundred scholars and theologians representing the world's communities of faith.

On September 2-4, 1993, the document was discussed by an assembly of religious and spiritual leaders meeting as part of the 1993 Parliament of the World's Religions in Chicago. Respected leaders from all the world's major faiths signed the declaration as individuals, agreeing that it represents an initial effort: a point of beginning for a world sorely in need of ethical consensus.

The Council for a Parliament of the World's Religions and the persons who have endorsed this text offer it to the world as an initial statement of those rules for living on which the world's religions agree.

THE WORLD IS IN AGONY.

The agony is so pervasive and urgent that we are compelled to name its manifestations so that the depth of this pain may be made clear.

Peace eludes us . . . the planet is being destroyed . . . neighbors live in fear . . . women and men are estranged from each other . . . children die!

THIS IS ABHORRENT!

We condemn the abuses of Earth's ecosystems.

We condemn the poverty that stifles life's potential; the hunger that weakens the human body; the economic disparities that threaten so many families with ruin.

We condemn the social disarray of the nations; the disregard for justice which pushes citizens to the margin; the anarchy overtaking our communities; and the insane death of children from violence. In particular we condemn aggression and hatred in the name of religion.

BUT THIS AGONY NEED NOT BE.

It need not be because the basis for an ethic already exists. This ethic offers the possibility of a better individual and global order, and leads individuals away from despair and societies away from chaos.

We are women and men who have embraced the precepts and practices of the world's religions:

We affirm that a common set of core values is found in the teachings of the religions, and that these form the basis of a global ethic.

We affirm that this truth is already known, but yet to be lived in heart and action.

We affirm that there is an irrevocable, unconditional norm for all areas of life, for families and communities, for races, nations, and religions. There already exist ancient guidelines for human behavior which are found in the teachings of the religions of the world and which are the condition for a sustainable world order.

WE DECLARE:

We are interdependent. Each of us depends on the well-being of the whole, and so we have respect for the community of living beings, for people, animals, and plants, and for the preservation of Earth, the air, water and soil.

We take individual responsibility for all we do. All our decisions, actions, and failures to act have consequences.

We must treat others as we wish others to treat us. We make a commitment to respect life and dignity, individuality and diversity, so that every person is treated humanely, without exception. We must have patience and acceptance. We must be able to forgive, learning from the past but never allowing ourselves to be enslaved by memories of hate. Opening our hearts to one another, we must sink our narrow differences for the cause of the world community, practicing a culture of solidarity and relatedness.

We consider humankind our family. We must strive to be kind and generous. We must not live for ourselves alone, but should also serve others, never forgetting the children, the aged, the poor, the suffering, the disabled, the refugees, and the lonely. No person should ever be considered or treated as a second-class citizen, or be exploited in any way whatsoever. There should be equal partnership between men and women. We must not commit any kind of sexual immorality. We must put behind us all forms of domination or abuse.

We commit ourselves to a culture of non-violence, respect, justice, and peace. We shall not oppress, injure, torture, or kill other human beings, forsaking violence as a means of settling differences.

We must strive for a just social and economic order, in which everyone has an equal chance to reach full potential as a human being. We must speak and act truthfully and with compassion, dealing fairly with all, and avoiding prejudice and hatred. We must not steal. We must move beyond the dominance of greed for power, prestige, money, and consumption to make a just and peaceful world.

Earth cannot be changed for the better unless the consciousness of individuals is changed first. We pledge to increase our awareness by disciplining our minds, by meditation, by prayer, or by positive thinking. Without risk and a readiness to sacrifice there can be no fundamental change in our situation. Therefore we commit our-selves to this global ethic, to understanding one another, and to socially beneficial, peace-fostering, and nature-friendly ways of life.

We invite all people, whether religious or not, to do the same.

The Earth Charter

In a 12-year grassroots drafting process, thousands of people in some 56 countries gathered in cities, villages, meeting halls, schools and in open-air settings to weave their shared dreams for a better world into the Earth Charter. The Earth Charter is a "Declaration of Interdependence" that outlines principles for respecting and caring for the community of life, social and economic justice, the environment, democracy, nonviolence, and peace. These principles are not just idealistic visions or dreams. Formally launched in September 2001, the Earth Charter constitutes a practical guide for "we the people" to create a more livable and equitable world.

PREAMBLE

We stand at a critical moment in Earth's history, a time when humanity must choose its future. As the world becomes increasingly interdependent and fragile, the future at once holds great peril and great promise. To move forward we must recognize that in the midst of a magnificent diversity of cultures and life forms we are one human family and one Earth community with a common destiny. We must join together to bring forth a sustainable global society founded on respect for nature, universal human rights, economic justice, and a culture of peace. Towards this end, it is imperative that we, the peoples of Earth, declare our responsibility to one another, to the greater community of life, and to future generations.

EARTH, OUR HOME

Humanity is part of a vast evolving universe. Earth, our home, is alive with a unique community of life. The forces of nature make existence a demanding and uncertain adventure, but Earth has provided the conditions essential to life's evolution. The resilience of the community of life and the well-being of humanity depend upon preserving a healthy biosphere with all its ecological systems, a rich variety of plants and animals, fertile soils, pure waters, and clean air. The global environment with its finite resources is a common concern of all peoples. The protection of Earth's vitality, diversity, and beauty is a sacred trust.

THE GLOBAL SITUATION

The dominant patterns of production and consumption are causing environmental devastation, the depletion of resources, and a massive extinction of species. Communities are being undermined. The benefits of development are not shared equitably and the gap between rich and poor is widening. Injustice, poverty, ignorance, and violent conflict are widespread and the cause of great suffering. An unprecedented rise in human population has overburdened ecological and social systems. The foundations of global security are threatened. These trends are perilous—but not inevitable.

THE CHALLENGES AHEAD

The choice is ours: form a global partnership to care for Earth and one another or risk the destruction of ourselves and the diversity of life. Fundamental changes are needed in our values, institutions, and ways of living. We must realize that when basic needs have been met, human development is primarily about being more, not having more. We have the knowledge and technology to provide for all and to reduce our impacts on the environment. The emergence of a global civil society is creating new opportunities to build a democratic and humane world. Our environmental, economic, political, social, and spiritual challenges are interconnected, and together we can forge inclusive solutions.

UNIVERSAL RESPONSIBILITY

To realize these aspirations, we must decide to live with a sense of universal responsibility, identifying ourselves with the whole Earth community as well as our local communities. We are at once citizens of different nations and of one world in which the local and global are linked. Everyone shares responsibility for the present and future well-being of the human family and the larger living world. The spirit of human solidarity and kinship with all life is strengthened when we live with reverence for the mystery of being, gratitude for the gift of life, and humility regarding the human place in nature.

We urgently need a shared vision of basic values to provide an ethical foundation for the emerging world community. Therefore, together in hope we affirm the following interdependent principles for a sustainable way of life as a common standard by which the conduct of all individuals, organizations, businesses, governments, and transnational institutions is to be guided and assessed.

PRINCIPLES

I. Respect and Care for the Community of Life

1. Respect Earth and life in all its diversity.
   a. Recognize that all beings are interdependent and every form of life has value regardless of its worth to human beings.
   b. Affirm faith in the inherent dignity of all human beings and in the intellectual, artistic, ethical, and spiritual potential of humanity.

2. Care for the community of life with understanding, compassion, and love.
   a. Accept that with the right to own, manage, and use natural resources comes the duty to prevent environmental

harm and to protect the rights of people.

b. Affirm that with increased freedom, knowledge, and power comes increased responsibility to promote the common good.

3. Build democratic societies that are just, participatory, sustainable, and peaceful.

a. Ensure that communities at all levels guarantee human rights and fundamental freedoms and provide everyone an opportunity to realize his or her full potential.

b. Promote social and economic justice, enabling all to achieve a secure and meaningful livelihood that is ecologically responsible.

4. Secure Earth's bounty and beauty for present and future generations.

a. Recognize that the freedom of action of each generation is qualified by the needs of future generations.

b. Transmit to future generations values, traditions, and institutions that support the long-term flourishing of Earth's human and ecological communities.

In order to fulfill these four broad commitments, it is necessary to:

II. Ecological Integrity

5. Protect and restore the integrity of Earth's ecological systems, with special concern for biological diversity and the natural processes that sustain life.

a. Adopt at all levels sustainable development plans and regulations that make environmental conservation and rehabilitation integral to all development initiatives.

b. Establish and safeguard viable nature and biosphere reserves, including wild lands and marine areas, to protect Earth's life support systems, maintain biodiversity, and preserve our natural heritage.

    c. Promote the recovery of endangered species and ecosystems.

    d. Control and eradicate non-native or genetically modified organisms harmful to native species and the environment, and prevent introduction of such harmful organisms.

    e. Manage the use of renewable resources such as water, soil, forest products, and marine life in ways that do not exceed rates of regeneration and that protect the health of ecosystems.

    f. Manage the extraction and use of non-renewable resources such as minerals and fossil fuels in ways that minimize depletion and cause no serious environmental damage.

6. Prevent harm as the best method of environmental protection and, when knowledge is limited, apply a precautionary approach.

    a. Take action to avoid the possibility of serious or irreversible environmental harm even when scientific knowledge is incomplete or inconclusive.

    b. Place the burden of proof on those who argue that a proposed activity will not cause significant harm, and make the responsible parties liable for environmental harm.

    c. Ensure that decision making addresses the cumulative, long-term, indirect, long distance, and global consequences of human activities.

    d. Prevent pollution of any part of the environment and allow no build-up of radioactive, toxic, or other hazardous substances.

    e. Avoid military activities damaging to the environment.

7. Adopt patterns of production, consumption, and reproduction that safeguard Earth's regenerative capacities, human rights, and community well-being.

    a. Reduce, reuse, and recycle the materials used in production and consumption systems, and ensure that residual waste can be assimilated by ecological systems.

    b. Act with restraint and efficiency when using energy, and

rely increasingly on renewable energy sources such as solar and wind.

c. Promote the development, adoption, and equitable transfer of environmentally sound technologies.

d. Internalize the full environmental and social costs of goods and services in the selling price, and enable consumers to identify products that meet the highest social and environmental standards.

e. Ensure universal access to health care that fosters reproductive health and responsible reproduction.

f. Adopt lifestyles that emphasize the quality of life and material sufficiency in a finite world.

8. Advance the study of ecological sustainability and promote the open exchange and wide application of the knowledge acquired.

a. Support international scientific and technical cooperation on sustainability, with special attention to the needs of developing nations.

b. Recognize and preserve the traditional knowledge and spiritual wisdom in all cultures that contribute to environmental protection and human well-being.

c. Ensure that information of vital importance to human health and environmental protection, including genetic information, remains available in the public domain.

III. Social and Economic Justice

9. Eradicate poverty as an ethical, social, and environmental imperative.

a. Guarantee the right to potable water, clean air, food security, uncontaminated soil, shelter, and safe sanitation, allocating the national and international resources required.

b. Empower every human being with the education and resources to secure a sustainable livelihood, and provide social security and safety nets for those who are unable to support themselves.

c. Recognize the ignored, protect the vulnerable, serve those who suffer, and enable them to develop their capacities and to pursue their aspirations.

10. Ensure that economic activities and institutions at all levels promote human development in an equitable and sustainable manner.

a. Promote the equitable distribution of wealth within nations and among nations.

b. Enhance the intellectual, financial, technical, and social resources of developing nations, and relieve them of onerous international debt.

c. Ensure that all trade supports sustainable resource use, environmental protection, and progressive labor standards.

d. Require multinational corporations and international financial organizations to act transparently in the public good, and hold them accountable for the consequences of their activities.

11. Affirm gender equality and equity as prerequisites to sustainable development and ensure universal access to education, health care, and economic opportunity.

a. Secure the human rights of women and girls and end all violence against them.

b. Promote the active participation of women in all aspects of economic, political, civil, social, and cultural life as full and equal partners, decision makers, leaders, and beneficiaries.

c. Strengthen families and ensure the safety and loving nurture of all family members.

12. Uphold the right of all, without discrimination, to a natural and social environment supportive of human dignity, bodily health, and spiritual well-being, with special attention to the rights of indigenous peoples and minorities.

a. Eliminate discrimination in all its forms, such as that based on race, color, sex, sexual orientation, religion, language, and national, ethnic or social origin.

b. Affirm the right of indigenous peoples to their spirituality, knowledge, lands and resources and to their related practice of sustainable livelihoods.

c. Honor and support the young people of our communities, enabling them to fulfill their essential role in creating sustainable societies.

d. Protect and restore outstanding places of cultural and spiritual significance.

IV. Democracy, Nonviolence, and Peace

13. Strengthen democratic institutions at all levels, and provide transparency and accountability in governance, inclusive participation in decision making, and access to justice.

a. Uphold the right of everyone to receive clear and timely information on environmental matters and all development plans and activities which are likely to affect them or in which they have an interest.

b. Support local, regional and global civil society, and promote the meaningful participation of all interested individuals and organizations in decision making.

c. Protect the rights to freedom of opinion, expression, peaceful assembly, association, and dissent.

d. Institute effective and efficient access to administrative and independent judicial procedures, including remedies and redress for environmental harm and the threat of such harm.

e. Eliminate corruption in all public and private institutions.

f. Strengthen local communities, enabling them to care for their environments, and assign environmental responsibilities to the levels of government where they can be carried out most effectively.

14. Integrate into formal education and life-long learning the knowledge, values, and skills needed for a sustainable way of life.
    a. Provide all, especially children and youth, with educational opportunities that empower them to contribute actively to sustainable development.
    b. Promote the contribution of the arts and humanities as well as the sciences in sustainability education.
    c. Enhance the role of the mass media in raising awareness of ecological and social challenges.
    d. Recognize the importance of moral and spiritual education for sustainable living.

15. Treat all living beings with respect and consideration.
    a. Prevent cruelty to animals kept in human societies and protect them from suffering.
    b. Protect wild animals from methods of hunting, trapping, and fishing that cause extreme, prolonged, or avoidable suffering.
    c. Avoid or eliminate to the full extent possible the taking or destruction of non-targeted species.

16. Promote a culture of tolerance, nonviolence, and peace.
    a. Encourage and support mutual understanding, solidarity, and cooperation among all peoples and within and among nations.
    b. Implement comprehensive strategies to prevent violent conflict and use collaborative problem solving to manage and resolve environmental conflicts and other disputes.
    c. Demilitarize national security systems to the level of a non-provocative defense posture, and convert military resources to peaceful purposes, including ecological restoration.
    d. Eliminate nuclear, biological, and toxic weapons and other weapons of mass destruction.
    e. Ensure that the use of orbital and outer space supports environmental protection and peace.

f. Recognize that peace is the wholeness created by right relationships with oneself, other persons, other cultures, other life, Earth, and the larger whole of which all are a part.

THE WAY FORWARD

As never before in history, common destiny beckons us to seek a new beginning. Such renewal is the promise of these Earth Charter principles. To fulfill this promise, we must commit ourselves to adopt and promote the values and objectives of the Charter.

This requires a change of mind and heart. It requires a new sense of global interdependence and universal responsibility. We must imaginatively develop and apply the vision of a sustainable way of life locally, nationally, regionally, and globally. Our cultural diversity is a precious heritage and different cultures will find their own distinctive ways to realize the vision. We must deepen and expand the global dialogue that generated the Earth Charter, for we have much to learn from the ongoing collaborative search for truth and wisdom.

Life often involves tensions between important values. This can mean difficult choices. However, we must find ways to harmonize diversity with unity, the exercise of freedom with the common good, short-term objectives with long-term goals. Every individual, family, organization, and community has a vital role to play. The arts, sciences, religions, educational institutions, media, businesses, nongovernmental organizations, and governments are all called to offer creative leadership. The partnership of government, civil society, and business is essential for effective governance.

In order to build a sustainable global community, the nations of the world must renew their commitment to the United Nations, fulfill their obligations under existing international agreements, and support the implementation of Earth Charter principles with an international legally binding instrument on environment and development.

Let ours be a time remembered for the awakening of a new reverence for life, the firm resolve to achieve sustainability, the quickening of the struggle for justice and peace, and the joyful celebration of life.

The Russell-Einstein Manifesto

The Russell-Einstein Manifesto was issued on 9 July 1955 in London. The manifesto invited scientists around the world to ward off the danger of nuclear weapons from ever being used again. The signatories also made an urgent appeal to all governments to understand that humanity had entered a new era in which conflicts would have to be settled by peaceful means, "for there can be no winners in a nuclear war." In addition to Bertrand Russell and Albert Einstein, the following distinguished scientists also signed the Russell-Einstein Manifesto: Max Born, Perry W. Bridgman, Leopold Infeld, Frédéric Joliot-Curie, Herman J. Muller, Linus Pauling, Cecil F. Powell, Joseph Rotblat and Hideki Yukawa.

In the tragic situation which confronts humanity, we feel that scientists should assemble in conference to appraise the perils that have arisen as a result of the development of weapons of mass destruction, and to discuss a resolution in the spirit of the appended draft.

We are speaking on this occasion, not as members of this or that nation, continent, or creed, but as human beings, members of the species Man, whose continued existence is in doubt. The world is full of conflicts; and, overshadowing all minor conflicts, the titanic struggle between Communism and anti-Communism.

Almost everybody who is politically conscious has strong feelings about one or more of these issues; but we want you, if you can, to set aside such feelings and consider yourselves only as members of a biological species which has had a remarkable history, and whose disappearance none of us can desire.

We shall try to say no single word which should appeal to one group rather than to another. All, equally, are in peril, and, if the peril is understood, there is hope that they may collectively avert it.

We have to learn to think in a new way. We have to learn to ask ourselves, not what steps can be taken to give military victory to whatever group we prefer, for there no longer are such steps; the question we have to ask ourselves is: what steps can be taken to prevent a military contest of which the issue must be disastrous to all parties?

The general public, and even many men in positions of authority, have not realized what would be involved in a war with nuclear bombs. The general public still thinks in terms of the obliteration of cities. It is understood that the new bombs are more powerful than the old, and that, while one A-bomb could obliterate Hiroshima, one H-bomb could obliterate the largest cities, such as London, New York, and Moscow.

No doubt in an H-bomb war great cities would be obliterated. But this is one of the minor disasters that would have to be faced. If everybody in London, New York, and Moscow were exterminated, the world might, in the course of a few centuries, recover from the blow. But we now know, especially since the Bikini test, that nuclear bombs can gradually spread destruction over a very much wider area than had been supposed.

It is stated on very good authority that a bomb can now be manufactured which will be 2,500 times as powerful as that which destroyed Hiroshima. Such a bomb, if exploded near the ground or under water, sends radioactive particles into the upper air. They sink gradually and reach the surface of the earth in the form of a deadly dust or rain. It was this dust which infected the Japanese fishermen and their catch of fish. No one knows how widely such lethal radio-active particles might be diffused, but the best authorities are unanimous in saying that a war with H-bombs might possibly put an end to the human race. It is feared that if many H-bombs are used there will be universal death, sudden only for a minority, but for the majority a slow torture of disease and disintegration.

Many warnings have been uttered by eminent men of science

and by authorities in military strategy. None of them will say that the worst results are certain. What they do say is that these results are possible, and no one can be sure that they will not be realized. We have not yet found that the views of experts on this question depend in any degree upon their politics or prejudices. They depend only, so far as our researches have revealed, upon the extent of the particular expert's knowledge. We have found that the men who know most are the most gloomy.

Here, then, is the problem which we present to you, stark and dreadful and inescapable: Shall we put an end to the human race; or shall mankind renounce war? People will not face this alternative because it is so difficult to abolish war.

The abolition of war will demand distasteful limitations of national sovereignty. But what perhaps impedes understanding of the situation more than anything else is that the term "mankind" feels vague and abstract. People scarcely realize in imagination that the danger is to themselves and their children and their grandchildren, and not only to a dimly apprehended humanity. They can scarcely bring themselves to grasp that they, individually, and those whom they love are in imminent danger of perishing agonizingly. And so they hope that perhaps war may be allowed to continue provided modern weapons are prohibited.

This hope is illusory. Whatever agreements not to use H-bombs had been reached in time of peace, they would no longer be considered binding in time of war, and both sides would set to work to manufacture H-bombs as soon as war broke out, for, if one side manufactured the bombs and the other did not, the side that manufactured them would inevitably be victorious.

Although an agreement to renounce nuclear weapons as part of a general reduction of armaments would not afford an ultimate solution, it would serve certain important purposes. First, any agreement between East and West is to the good in so far as it tends to diminish tension. Second, the abolition of thermonuclear weapons, if each side believed that the other had carried it out sincerely, would lessen the fear of a sudden attack in the style of Pearl Harbour, which at present keeps both sides in a state of nervous apprehension. We should, therefore, welcome such an agreement though only as a first step.

Most of us are not neutral in feeling, but, as human beings, we have to remember that, if the issues between East and West are to be decided in any manner that can give any possible satisfaction to anybody, whether Communist or anti-Communist, whether Asian or European or American, whether White or Black, then these issues must not be decided by war. We should wish this to be understood, both in the East and in the West.

There lies before us, if we choose, continual progress in happiness, knowledge, and wisdom. Shall we, instead, choose death, because we cannot forget our quarrels? We appeal as human beings to human beings: Remember your humanity, and forget the rest. If you can do so, the way lies open to a new Paradise; if you cannot, there lies before you the risk of universal death.

RESOLUTION:

We invite this Congress, and through it the scientists of the world and the general public, to subscribe to the following resolution:

"In view of the fact that in any future world war nuclear weapons will certainly be employed, and that such weapons threaten the continued existence of mankind, we urge the governments of the world to realize, and to acknowledge publicly, that their purpose cannot be furthered by a world war, and we urge them, consequently, to find peaceful means for the settlement of all matters of dispute between them."

Max Born
Perry W. Bridgman
Albert Einstein
Leopold Infeld
Frederic Joliot-Curie
Herman J. Muller

Linus Pauling
Cecil F. Powell
Joseph Rotblat
Bertrand Russell
Hideki Yukawa

Appeal to End the Nuclear Weapons Threat to Humanity and All Life

Addressed to all leaders of the world, but particularly the leaders of the nuclear weapons states, the Appeal to End the Nuclear Weapons Threat to Humanity and All Life was launched by the Nuclear Age Peace Foundation in 2000. The Appeal urges the world's leaders to take practical steps for the benefit of humanity and all life, particularly de-alerting all nuclear weapons; commencing negotiations for elimination of all nuclear weapons; and reallocating resources from maintaining nuclear arsenals to improving human health, education, and welfare. The Appeal has now been signed by many prominent leaders of our time, including Jimmy Carter, Mikhail Gorbachev, Archbishop Desmond Tutu, the XIVth Dalai Lama, Queen Noor of Jordan, Coretta Scott King, and Muhammad Ali. Among its signers are 38 Nobel Laureates, including 15 Nobel Peace Laureates.

We cannot hide from the threat that nuclear weapons pose to humanity and all life. These are not ordinary weapons, but instruments of mass annihilation that could destroy civilization and end life on Earth.

Nuclear weapons are morally and legally unjustifiable. They destroy indiscriminately—soldiers and civilians; men, women and children; the aged and the newly born; the healthy and the infirm.

The obligation to achieve nuclear disarmament "in all its aspects," as unanimously affirmed by the International Court of Justice, is at the heart of the Non-Proliferation Treaty.

More than ten years have now passed since the end of the Cold War, and yet nuclear weapons continue to cloud humanity's future.

The only way to assure that nuclear weapons will not be used again is to abolish them.

We, therefore, call upon the leaders of the nations of the world and, in particular, the leaders of the nuclear weapons states to act now for the benefit of all humanity by taking the following steps:

- Ratify the Comprehensive Test Ban Treaty and reaffirm commitments to the 1972 Anti-Ballistic Missile Treaty.

- De-alert all nuclear weapons and de-couple all nuclear warheads from their delivery vehicles

- Declare policies of No First Use of nuclear weapons against other nuclear weapons states and policies of No Use against non-nuclear weapons states.

- Commence good faith negotiations to achieve a Nuclear Weapons Convention requiring the phased elimination of all nuclear weapons, with provisions for effective verification and enforcement.

- Reallocate resources from the tens of billions of dollars currently being spent for maintaining nuclear arsenals to improving human health, education and welfare throughout the world.

Authors

HAFSAT ABIOLA

Hafsat Abiola is a young human rights and democracy activist from Lagos, Nigeria. She received her B.A. from Harvard University. Her work for the rights of women and children in Nigeria and in other African countries has elicited recognition and praise throughout the world. Hafsat founded and directs an organization called the Kudirat Initiative for Democracy (KIND), named for her mother, to continue the legacy of her parents, who fought tirelessly for democracy in Nigeria. She has received many honors for her work, including the 2001 Distinguished Peace Leadership Award of the Nuclear Age Peace Foundation.

ELISE BOULDING

A Professor Emerita of sociology at Dartmouth College, Elise Boulding was born in Oslo, Norway, in 1920. She earned a Ph.D. at the University of Michigan in 1969. A former member of the International Jury of UNESCO (1981-1987), she led the move to establish the U.S. Peace Institute in 1984. She is also a founder of the International Peace Research Association and a distinguished member of the Religious Society of Friends (Quakers). Ms. Boulding has been the recipient of numerous honors for her achievements as a scholar and activist in the areas of peace and world order, democracy, and women in society. In 1973, she received the Douglass

College Distinguished Achievement Award. She was nominated for the Nobel Peace Prize in 1990, and has authored 19 books and hundreds of chapters and articles.

BILL CANE

Bill Cane is a former Professor at Graduate Theological Union in Berkeley, California. He is presently executive director of IF, a non-profit group that sponsors life-giving alternatives in the US and in the Third World. He is also the author of *Through Crisis to Freedom* and *Circles of Hope*, and editor of the quarterly *Integrities*.

ADAM CURLE

Adam Curle has held chairs in psychology, education and development studies at the universities of Exeter, Harvard, and Ghana. From 1973-78 he was the first Professor of Peace Studies at the University of Bradford. He has worked as a mediator and promoter of peace in India and Pakistan, Nigeria/Biafra, South Africa, Zimbabwe, Northern Ireland and Sri Lanka, and helped to set up peace groups and trauma counseling facilities in Bosnia and Croatia. He is active in the Religious Society of Friends (Quakers) and reveres the teaching of the Dalai Lama of Tibet.

DALAI LAMA

His Holiness the Fourteenth Dalai Lama, Tenzin Gyatso, is the spiritual and temporal leader of the Tibetan people. He is the recipient of the Nobel Peace Prize, the Nuclear Age Peace Foundation's Distinguished Peace Leadership Award and many other honors. He is the author of *Freedom in Exile, The Autobiography of the Dalai Lama, The Art of Happiness*, and numerous other books and articles.

RICHARD FALK

Richard Falk, J.S.D., is chair of the Nuclear Age Peace Foundation. He is Albert G. Milbank Professor Emeritus of International

Law and Policy at Princeton University and a Distinguished Visiting Professor at the University of California at Santa Barbara. Professor Falk has authored over forty books, written numerous chapters in books and uncounted articles in the fields of international relations, international law, and human rights. Among many other positions, he has been a congressional fellow and vice president of the American Political Science Association, a member of the Council on Foreign Relations, and a member of the editorial board for *The Nation*.

FREDERICK FRANCK

Frederick Franck is an oral surgeon and artist whose lifelong artistic efforts have transcended national boundaries and touched a core of human compassion. From 1958 to 1961, Franck worked on Albert Schweitzer's medical staff. Franck was inspired by Schweitzer, Pope John Paul XXIII, and Daisetz T. Suzuki to build Pacem in Terris, converting the ruin of an 18th Century watermill in Warwick, New York, into a trans-religious sanctuary, a work of art in many media and a tiny oasis of quiet and sanity. At the age of 85, Franck is author of many books, including *What Does it Mean to Be Human? Reverence for Life Reaffirmed* (St. Martin's Press, 2000). He has received many honors for his work, including the 2001 World Citizenship Award of the Nuclear Age Peace Foundation.

GENE KNUDSEN HOFFMAN

Gene Knudsen Hoffman was born in Los Angeles, California in 1919. She has had careers in radio, theater, writing, psychology, and peace. She is a member of the Religious Society of Friends (Quakers) and is a pastoral counselor. In 1980, she began writing about Compassionate Listening as a healing and peace process. In 1996, Compassionate Listening became a full-fledged program for domestic (US) conflicts and divisive public differences. It has also been used in the Middle East.

BARBARA MARX HUBBARD

Barbara Marx Hubbard is an author, speaker and social innovator, now serving as President of the Foundation for Conscious Evolution. In 1984, 200 delegates signed a petition to place her name in nomination for the Vice Presidency of the United States on the Democratic ticket, on the strength of her proposal to place a "Peace Room" in the White House. A graduate of Bryn Mawr College, cum laude, with a B.A. in Political Science, she is a founding director of several organizations, including The World Future Society, The Foundation for the Future, and the Association for Global New Thought. She has written several books, including *Conscious Evolution*.

DAISAKU IKEDA

Daisaku Ikeda is President of Soka Gakkai International (SGI) and has been instrumental in establishing various institutions related to peace, culture, and education, all reflecting Buddhist principles. Mr. Ikeda was an early proponent of citizen diplomacy, meeting with leaders in China and the Soviet Union from the early 1970s. Mr. Ikeda has published works in Japanese and 25 other languages on subjects ranging from Buddhist philosophy to children's stories. His photographs taken during travels in Japan and abroad have been compiled into an exhibition, "Dialogue with Nature," shown around the world. Mr. Ikeda authors an annual peace proposal that is presented to the United Nations. He is the recipient of many honorary degrees and numerous awards, including the Nuclear Age Peace Foundation's 1999 World Citizenship Award.

FRANK K. KELLY

Frank K. Kelly has been a noted science fiction writer, a prize winning journalist, a soldier in World War II, a Nieman Fellow at Harvard University, a professor at Boston University, a speechwriter for Harry Truman, a special assistant to the US Senate Majority Leader, a leader in the campaign that created the US Institute of Peace, a vice president of the Center for the Study of Democratic Institutions, and a founder and Senior Vice President of the Nuclear Age Peace Foundation. He has written nine books and uncounted articles.

CRAIG KIELBURGER

Craig Kielburger, a youthful human rights activist from Toronto, Canada, is an international spokesperson for children's rights. His efforts to end child labor abuses worldwide have earned Craig the respect and admiration of the international community. At the age of 12, Craig founded Kids Can Free the Children, an organization dedicated to ending abusive child labor practices around the world. It is now the world's largest network of children helping children, with over 100,000 active youth in dozens of countries. Craig's first book, *Free the Children*, recounts his travels to help youth caught up in bonded labor and has been translated into seven languages. Craig also co-authored *Take Action!* with his brother Marc. He has received numerous awards and honors for his work, including the Nuclear Age Peace Foundation's 2001 Distinguished Peace Leadership Award.

MARC KIELBURGER

Marc Kielburger is a Harvard graduate and Rhodes Scholar in law at Oxford University. He is the co-founder of Leaders Today, an international organization that empowers youth through leadership programs on local, national, and international levels. He has led youth volunteer trips to Kenya, Ecuador, India, Thailand, and Nicaragua. He has visited numerous war-torn regions throughout the world, working with children affected by conflict, including Algeria, Bosnia, and the former Yugoslavia. He is the co-author of the book *Take Action!*, which was profiled on the Oprah Winfrey Show. Marc regularly hosts motivational skill-building workshops and seminars for youth across North America and has facilitated workshops for the United Nations and the State of the World Forum.

DAVID KRIEGER

David Krieger is a founder of the Nuclear Age Peace Foundation, and has served as President of the Foundation since 1982. He is the author of many studies of peace in the nuclear age and has lectured throughout the United States, Europe, and Asia on issues of peace, security, international law, and the abolition of nuclear weapons.

His most recent books are *The Poetry of Peace* (editor) and *Choose Hope, Your Role in Waging Peace in the Nuclear Age,* a dialogue with Japanese Buddhist leader Daisaku Ikeda. He serves as an advisor and board member of many peace and nuclear disarmament organizations throughout the world, and has received many honors for his work.

MAIREAD CORRIGAN MAGUIRE

Mairead Corrigan Maguire found herself in a leading position in the peace movement in the wake of a tragic event. On August 10, 1976 three children, two of her nephews and one of her nieces, were killed in Belfast by an IRA gunman's car whose driver had been shot dead by a British soldier. In the aftermath of these children's senseless deaths, Mairead Maguire, along with Betty Williams and Ciaran McKeown, organized the largest peace demonstrations in the history of Northern Ireland to demand an end to the violence. In 1976, Mairead Maguire and Betty Williams received the Nobel Peace Prize for their efforts. Maguire has been an outspoken advocate for non-violence and has worked ceaselessly with grassroots community groups to promote dialogue and understanding between the divided communities in Northern Ireland. She is a co-founder of Peace People, a recipient of the Norwegian People's Prize, the Nuclear Age Peace Foundation's Distinguished Peace Leadership Award, and an honorary doctorate degree from Yale University.

JOANNA MACY

Eco-philosopher Joanna Macy, Ph.D., is a scholar of Buddhism, general systems theory, and deep ecology. She is also a leading voice in movements for peace, justice, and a safe environment. Interweaving her scholarship and four decades of activism, she has created both a ground-breaking theoretical framework for a new paradigm of personal and social change, and a powerful workshop methodology for its application. She travels widely giving lectures, workshops, and trainings in North America, Europe, Asia, and Australia. She serves as adjunct professor to two graduate schools in the San Francisco Bay Area: the Starr King School for the Ministry, and the University of Creation Spirituality.

GEORGIANNA MOORE

Georgianna Moore (1927-2002), a theatre director most of her life, also wrote children's stories. *The Message of the Sunflowers* was written for Symposium 2000—World Peace through Reverence for Life, a Celebration of Albert Schweitzer and J.S. Bach, which was sponsored by Vanderbilt University and produced by Tennessee Players, Inc., the theatre company she co-founded with her husband, Thurston Moore.

ROBERT MULLER

Robert Muller served in the United Nations for thirty-eight years. Appointed assistant secretary-general by Perez de Cuellar, his last assignment at the UN was to organize the fortieth anniversary of the UN in 1985. An internationally known speaker and author, he is Chancellor Emeritus of the University for Peace established by the UN in Costa Rica. His books have been published in several languages. Muller is considered the father of global education. He has received the 1989 UNESCO Peace Education Prize, the 1993 International Albert Schweitzer Prize for Humanities, the 1994 Eleanor Roosevelt Man of Vision Award, and the 2002 World Citizenship Award of the Nuclear Age Peace Foundation.

QUEEN NOOR AL HUSSEIN

Educated at Princeton University, Queen Noor al Hussein earned a B.A. in architecture and urban planning. Marrying King Hussein in 1978, she tirelessly supported her husband's efforts for peace. She has promoted international exchange and understanding in Middle Eastern politics, Arab-Western relations and current global issues. Internationally, she has advocated environmental protection and ecotourism, and has long supported United Nations social programs for women and children. After Princess Diana's death, Queen Noor accepted the responsibility of Patron of the Landmine Survivors Network, in addition to her numerous global roles, which include Board Member of the World Wildlife Fund, Ambassador of Future Harvest, Chair of the Advisory Board of the Center for the Global South at American University, and Chair of the international Advisory Committee for the United Nations University International Leadership Academy. She received the Nuclear Age Peace Foundation's 2000 World Citizenship Award.

John Charles Polanyi

John Charles Polanyi received a Bachelor of Science degree from Manchester University in 1949 and a Ph.D. in 1952. Among many other awards, Polanyi received the Nobel Prize in Chemistry in 1986. He has been the recipient of honorary degrees from many universities. Polanyi was made an Officer of the Order of Canada in 1974, and a Companion of the Order of Canada in 1979. In addition to his scientific papers he has published approximately one hundred articles on science policy, on the control of armaments, and the impact of science on society. He has produced a film, *Concepts in Reaction Dynamics* (1970), and has co-edited a book, *The Dangers of Nuclear War* (1979).

Dennis Rivers

Dennis Rivers is a teacher and writer who lives in Santa Barbara, California. He holds degrees from the University of California at Los Angeles, the University of California at Santa Barbara, and the Vermont College Graduate Program. He has been teaching communication and conflict resolution classes for twenty years. His recent book on communication skills, *The Seven Challenges*, is available for free on the web at www.coopcomm.org, and available in print from Trafford Publishers (www.trafford.com).

Senator Douglas Roche

Senator Douglas Roche, O.C. is former Canadian Ambassador for Disarmament and former Chair of the United Nations Committee on Disarmament. He is the author of 15 books, including *Bread Not Bombs: A Political Agenda for Social Justice* (University of Alberta Press, 1999), and *The Ultimate Evil: The Fight to Ban Nuclear Weapons* (James Lorimer, 1997). He is Chairman of the Middle Powers Initiative and Chairman of the Canadian Pugwash Group. He was assisted in the preparation of his contribution to this book by his research assistant, Todd Martin, co-author of *Madness in the Multitude: Human Security and World Disorder* (Oxford University Press, 2001).

Sir Joseph Rotblat

Joseph Rotblat, born in Warsaw in 1908, obtained his M.A. from the Free University of Poland in 1932 and a doctorate in Physics from the University of Warsaw. In 1946 he co-founded the Atomic Scientists Association and in 1947 he organized "Atom Train," the first big exhibition on peaceful uses and against military applications of nuclear energy. Rotblat obtained his Ph.D. from the University of Liverpool in 1950 and his D.Sc. from the University of London in 1953. In 1955 Rotblat was one of the eleven signatories of the Russell-Einstein Manifesto.

In 1957 Rotblat founded the Pugwash Conferences on Science and World Affairs and became the first Secretary General of the organization. In 1958 he co-founded the Campaign for Nuclear Disarmament. Rotblat was the initiator and member of the preparatory committee and governing board of the Stockholm International Peace Research Institute. He helped establish a chair of Peace Studies at Bradford University. He is the author of over 300 publications, including 20 books, on nuclear and medical physics, radiation biology, control of nuclear weapons, disarmament, the Pugwash movement and the social responsibility of scientists. In 1995, Joseph Rotblat and the Pugwash Conferences were awarded the Nobel Prize for Peace. In 1997, Professor Rotblat received the Nuclear Age Peace Foundation's Lifetime Achievement Award.

ANDREW L. STRAUSS

Andrew L. Strauss is a professor of international law at Widener University School of Law. He earned his Bachelor of Arts at Princeton University's Woodrow Wilson School of Public and International Affairs and his Juris Doctorate at New York University School of Law. He has published in such venues as *Foreign Affairs*, the *Harvard Journal of International Law*, the *Stanford Journal of International Law* and the *International Herald Tribune*. He has lectured widely around the world.

ARCHBISHOP DESMOND TUTU

Archbishop Desmond Mpilo Tutu was born on October 7, 1931, in Klerksdorp, Transvaal, South Africa. From 1975 to 1976 he was the first black Dean at St. Mary's Cathedral in Johannesburg and, from 1976 to 1978, he was Bishop of Lesotho. In 1978 he became the first black General Secretary of the South African Council of Churches.

In 1984 he was awarded the Nobel Peace Prize, in recognition of his nonviolent campaign to limit international trade and investment activities in South Africa. He became Bishop of Johannesburg in 1985, and Archbishop of Cape Town and head of the Anglican Church in Southern Africa in 1986. After retiring as Archbishop in 1996 he became Chairperson of the Truth and Reconciliation Commission in South Africa, and presided over the traumatic revelation of the secrets of apartheid.

He has received awards, prizes and honorary degrees from all over the world, including the Nuclear Age Peace Foundation's Distinguished Peace Leadership Award.

LEAH WELLS

Leah Wells is Peace Education Coordinator for the Nuclear Age Peace Foundation. Since graduating from Georgetown University in 1998, she has become a global peace activist, dedicating herself to peace education. She has worked with nonprofit organizations such as the Center for Teaching Peace, the Fellowship of Reconciliation, and Voices in the Wilderness. In addition to teaching nonviolence as well as French and English, she has also worked with juvenile offenders and the Victim Offender Reconciliation Program (VORP).

Two thousand two hundred trade paperback copies of *Hope in a Dark Time* were printed by Capra Press in January 2003. One hundred copies have been numbered and signed by the editor and Archbishop Tutu. Twenty-six copies in slipcases were also lettered and signed.

About Capra Press

Capra Press was founded in 1969 by the late Noel Young. Among its authors have been Henry Miller, Ross Macdonald, Margaret Millar, Edward Abbey, Anais Nin, Raymond Carver, Ray Bradbury, and Lawrence Durrell. It is in this tradition that we present the new Capra Press: literary and mystery fiction, lifestyle and city books. Contact us. We welcome your comments.

815 De La Vina Street, Santa Barbara, CA 93101
805-892-2722; www.caprapress.com